Appetizer: Horse D'oovers

Your words were found and I ate them, and Your Word was to me the joy and rejoicing of my heart, for I am called by Your name, LORD, God of Hosts.

(Jeremiah 15:16)

Jesus/Yeshua is The True Bread of Life. The believing one who comes to Him through covenant will never go hungry or thirsty. He will provide all their needs of food, clothing, shelter and spiritual.

(StT John 6:35)

Cows and land are a part of my family's rich heritage.

During the 1960's, my two older sisters and I were raised by our paternal grandparents on their peanut/dairy farm. Grandpa Herman and Grandma Sarah were contented to spend their entire ninety something years of life, which included their seventy-one years of marriage, not far from the farm where grandpa had his upbringing and close to where grandma was reared on the land her dad staked claim in the 1895 Oklahoma land run.

Paula, Kay, and I had the distinction of attending our first through twelfth grades at the same school our grandparents got their learnin' before their graduation in 1929. It is noteworthy that we three girls had the one and the same high school English teacher who taught our parents.

A couple blocks away from the school stands the little old Methodist church built with the lumber our great paternal grandpa cut. As a kid, I loved ringing the church bell he hung upon the church's completion.

There was a certain security in my family's "if it ain't broke, don't fix it" way of doing things so disrupting the status quo was not the reason behind my many questions and lack of acceptance of a "because I said so" answer.

After having children of my own, I realized the need to apologize to my grandparents for the times I bucked their authority. Even though Grandpa said I wasn't "that bad," he probably thought the cows were easier to raise than having to deal with my persistent questioning.

Of course my attitude and actions were a reflection of my maturity level and not so much my cultural frame of reference of right or wrong. As a child, I didn't like 'having' to *work* so I was being a cranky nine year old during yet another cattle relocation. Daddy, Paula, and I would ride our horses on these moves that were needed in order to prevent the pasture's water source from drying up or over grazing.

On this particular drive, we were outnumbered by the cows one hundred twenty to three so the pressure to keep the cattle moving and off a busy highway was on. Daddy yelling his *instructions* didn't help my mood.

Out of the blue I noticed the occupant of a car with an out of state tag was taking a video of us. This took place in 1965 before most home movies recorded with audio and our rotary dial telephones had to be wired to the wall to work. Later as I was wondering why a stranger had wasted her valuable film on three horseback riders herding a bunch of cows, we got a call from our neighbors. Their young daughter had watched our cattle drive as we passed in front of their house and she wanted to know if we were playing "Rawhide."

It had never occurred to me that at a young age I was getting to do a real life cattle drive that this western television show's trail boss, Mr. Favor, only pretended to do. So I wasn't *working*; I was living the fantasy of a lot of kids across America.

This perspective reigned in my cantankerous attitude about work… well, for that day. A few years later, Grandpa would *lay hands* on me to *receive the gift* of his strong work ethic after I had thrown my hoe down and said I wasn't hoeing another peanut row. This spanking happened several

Something Stewing in a Cracked Pot

CULLING SACRED COWS FROM THE HERD WORD

Rhonda Archer

WESTBOW
PRESS®
A DIVISION OF THOMAS NELSON
& ZONDERVAN

WestBow Press books may be ordered through booksellers or by contacting:

WestBow Press
A Division of Thomas Nelson & Zondervan
1663 Liberty Drive
Bloomington, IN 47403
www.westbowpress.com
1 (866) 928-1240

Artwork by http://www.artofkleyn.com

Unless otherwise stated, Scripture quotations are taken from The One New Man Bible © 2011 William J. Morford. Used by permission of True Potential, Inc.

Non-quoted Scriptures labeled "StT" are for readers to "Season to Taste" with their translation flavor of choice.

ISBN: 978-1-9736-5681-4 (sc)
ISBN: 978-1-9736-5682-1 (hc)
ISBN: 978-1-9736-5680-7 (e)

Library of Congress Control Number: 2019902863

Print information available on the last page.

WestBow Press rev. date: 3/13/2019

To all cracked pots dissatisfied with Deception's scraps and hankerin' for the True Bread of Life revealed from the beginning in the Hebrew Scrolls.

Table of COWtents

summers past the first time I was to help with the weed control field chore of hoeing peanuts. Weeds compete with the peanuts for water, nutrients, and light and their invasion can greatly reduce a harvest. Timing the 'search and destroy mission' during the first six weeks after planting was crucial in order to give the young peanut plants a grace period to mature enough to survive any future nutrient battle.

Almost five but not big enough to get up on Silver without help from grandpa.

The large hoe in my small six years old hands targeted a lot of innocent peanut plants that first year as I walked between the rows inspecting a row up then turn around to scan another one on the way back. The "hoe-down" episode happened when I had matured to handle eight rows, four to my left and four to my right, at a time. Walking up and down, crisscrossing and stepping over several rows of peanuts to hoe nutrient thieves over an entire hot dusty field is sweaty, tedious, and tiring.

Grandpa may have *persuaded* me to pick up my hoe that day but picking up the mindset that work could actually strengthen my character and make me a productive member of society took a bit more *convincing*. It was Proverbs 12:11 and 2 Thessalonians 3:10 stating hard working farmers have plenty of food and anyone not **willing** to work shouldn't get the privilege of eating that helped my grasp; I really liked eating.

One lunch when we were teenagers, Kay was eating only a grapefruit while I was enjoying our standard meal of meat, mashed potatoes and milk gravy. After grandpa gave Kay his "you need to put meat on those bones" talk, he looked at me when he said, "I never have to worry about Rhonda *not* eating."

Come to think of it, all the food metaphors contained in God's Word might have something to do with my love for it. Jesus even said that He hangs out with the one who continually chews His flesh and drinks His blood. Which is a kind of strange way of saying we are to break His Word into small horse d'oovers (Or is it hors d'oeuvres?) to study, think about, then swallow it in order to properly absorb His Word so Its Wisdom steers our behavior.

Whoever wrote the book of Hebrews used milk and solid food to illustrate Biblical maturity levels. To nourish their spiritual life, newborn-*again* folks need the unadulterated spiritual milk of a mother's teaching (Old Testament Teachings) to help them out grow deceitfulness, pretentiousness, jealously and slander. A few newbies become contented to having someone else spoon feed them "grapefruit teachings" to satisfy their emotional needs instead of developing their life of faith by learning to eat for themselves. By settling for a grapefruit-mental-assent-to-Truth diet they risk being spiritual skinnies easily shaken when troubles blow in and get carried about by every windy myth or rules set up by men who have turned their backs on *didache'*, the doctrine authored by God Himself.

Jesus taught from the Torah; the only Teachings that can put meat on your spiritual bones and gives us strength to train *by practice* the discernment required for distinguishing Truth from its cross-breed look alike.

The aim of God's Teachings (Torah) is to *"love out of clean heart a good conscience and sincere faith, from which, when **some missed the mark** they turned away to **fruitless** talk wanting to be teachers of Torah (Teaching),* *although they understood neither what they were saying nor about what they were confidently insisting. But we **know** that the Torah (Teaching) is **good**..." (1 Timothy 1:5-8, **emphasis mine**)*

Contrary to popular belief, Paul does not give the Torah a bad rap in his first letter to Timothy but points out they share the understanding that God's Teaching is good. Both of them would've known the word for Torah, *yarah,* has the connotation of when a teacher's instructions "hits the mark" it has penetrated the heart similar to an arrow hitting its target.

Ouch! I guess Truth does hurt.

In Matthew 24:4, Jesus warns that we are not to be deceived by fancy talking *bad shots* who missed the mark and won't get to enter His Kingdom with the ones *on the mark* who **do** His Father's will.

Proverbs 1:5-9 can help our aim. Succulent wisdom starts with planting reverence for the LORD. Only fools despise the instructions and self-discipline required to grow in knowledge of His Truth.

Along with the victor's garland of grace on the head, kingly chains and pendants will hang around the neck of anyone willing to listen up to their Father's Instructions and stop rejecting their *mother's teachings* (Torah).

The recipe instructions in Deuteronomy 14:2 of not cooking a goat in its mother's milk ties a *mother's teaching* (Torah) with milk. Boiling *deception* with Torah not only toughens the meat of God's Word but makes it *steer*-ile.

For any city folk who might not know, a bull becomes a *steer* (sterile) when his "ability to reproduce life" is cut off through castration. Farmers use this method to make bulls easier to control. That's why this farm girl can see how teachers who say no-one needs to keep the Word of Life have led many into the error of ***steer***-ile beliefs by depriving them of the power to bear fruit.

The sheer number of denominations that exist today would seem to contradict my premise that de-*seeded* fruits don't multiply. Unless you take into account the church splits after a few stubborn old goats butted heads then I can still maintain ***steer***-ile beliefs don't multiply; they *divide.*

Mostly we think of a "stubborn old goat" as someone set in their ways and are very resistant to change but goats were linked with deception in Genesis 27:16-17 and 37: 31. Rebecca used *goat* hair and meat to help her son deceive his dad, Isaac, into thinking Jacob was Esau to get the first born blessing. This deception's payback would pierce Jacob's heart when his oldest sons used blood from a *goat* to trick him into thinking Joseph was dead.

"Brothers" are still around who like to twist the Truth with the aim of leading God's chosen into the ditch. Oh they will be protesting on the Day of Judgment that they prophesied, drove out demons, did miracles all in His Name but no amount of pleading on their part will make Jesus pencil their names into His Book of Life. Jesus will banish from His presence those who disregarded His commands and say He never knew them.

Naturally, Jesus has a mental awareness of every person but according to Matthew 7:21-23, He will cull anyone who has an utter disregard for His written Word and does not have the covenant right (similar to wedding vows) to take His Name.

Jesus assures us in John 14:12-15 that anyone who believes in Him as Savior would **do** the things that He was **do**-ing; and **do** even greater things than what He did because He was going to the One Who does not change but remains faithful to His covenant with us. That is why whatever we, as His representatives, ask in His Name He will **do** so our Father is glorified and His Son celebrated. **If we really love Him, we would happily keep and obey His commandments**.

I didn't personally count all the verses with "Thus saith the LORD;" but there were too many to quote here. I had trouble figuring out which scriptures to cull since in my eyes none could be deemed inferior. I decided to cook from scratch using what I could decipher of the original word meanings to make my own flavorful paraphrase then garnish them with "StT" so y'all can *"Season to Taste"* test everything using the biblical spice (translation) of your choice.

Based on Revelation 5:8, *Stirring the Golden Prayer Pot* at the end of each serving is my way of adding seasoning to heaven's golden pot full of prayers of the people who belong to the One Who sits on the Throne.

Even though our Father loves us personally, He mixes more than just our prayers together. Those thoughts of peace and a future the LORD promised to a Hebraic people in Jeremiah 29:11? God had spoken those words to an entire nation expecting each citizen to do their part for the future and purpose of their country. If we don't take into account that the Hebrew language was more relational than individualistic we will miss what He meant.

Farmers get it. Working together is part of farm life. It takes all available hands to prevent any crop loss when harvest time arrives. Probably why Jesus spoke of needing more people to follow Him in the family business.

God started it all by putting His Image bearer in the Garden of Eden to take care of and farm its land. Being the Second Adam may have been one reason Jesus grew up on the Nazareth Village Farm, referenced Himself as the True Vine, His Father the *Farmer* and why His parables were relatable to the agrarian culture of His listeners. (StT Luke 10:2; John 15:1; Genesis 2:15; Mark 4:27; Matthew 20:1)

Although there are many verses containing agricultural terms, the conversation between Jesus and Peter mentioning a farm fowl probably shouldn't be considered one of them. (StT Matthew 26:31-35; Mark 14:27-31; Luke 22:31-34; John 13:36-38)

Satan had received a go ahead to his request of testing Peter like a farmer separates wheat from its husks. Even though Peter would stumble in his faith, Jesus had already prayed that he would make a quick recovery and be the support that plants down his brothers' faith. To Peter's protest that he would go with the Lord even to prison or death, Jesus replied that before the **cock calls** on that very day, Peter would say three times that he didn't know Him.

The well-established interpretation is that Peter would deny Jesus three times before a rooster crowed. However from what I surmise of the inner workings of first century customs and culture, chickens were not allowed inside Jerusalem's walls in order to prevent this dirty bird from entering and defiling the Temple. Granted, early in the morning sounds travel further so a rooster might've been heard crowing in the distance but it would have to have been a *fur* piece from where Jesus stood in the Temple.

After looking up the Greek word for cock in a Strong's Concordance, I found *alektor* can be either a rooster or a man. The Hebrew word for cock didn't help clear things up like I had hoped. Turns out that *gever,* can mean a rooster or a man also.

I decided the Greek word, *phoneo,* describing what the *alektor* was doing might help with answering which came first, the chicken or the egg? I mean the rooster or the man? *Phoneo*, translated crows or calls, has a meaning to call out for, to address in words or by name, in order to imitate. If we can conclude a rooster doesn't use words or isn't calling for us to imitate him, then *alektor* is referencing a man.

The Gospel writers didn't bother explaining because their first century readers would actually know this particular man was a temple gatekeeper responsible for unlocking the Temple's gates every morning. (StT 1 Chronicles 9:27)

Anyone living in Jerusalem during the time of these events could've heard for themselves this priestly Temple Crier's early morning hour call for:

"All the cohanim (priests) prepare to sacrifice."

"All the Leviim (Levites) to their stations."

"All the Israelites come to worship."

Wow! It seems Jesus already knew that hearing the gatekeeper's call would be more convicting than a mere rooster sounding off by pointing out that Peter:

a. Wasn't going to have to die. (Only Jesus would have to be the sacrifice to restore the Covenant Way to the Father.)

b. Would abandon his station. (Jesus never abandons us.)

c. Would fail to even give Jesus 'lip service.' (Jesus saves those who approach God through Him and He lives forever in the presence of God to be their advocate.)

After all of Peter's crowing he would give his life for Him, Jesus encouraged Peter not to let what He just told him about his three time denial to trouble his heart and throw him off the trail of His Way. (StT Luke 22:31-34; John 14:1)

Lacking a Jewish mindset of how things were done at the Temple in the first century is one reason generations of believers would give a rooster top billing over a gatekeeper. Still, this way big interpretation discrepancy sparked my curiosity like never before.

If Proverbs 25:2 is saying God conceals revelation in His Word just to delight in watching persistent truth seekers joyfully discovering those hidden treasures of wisdom, I was going to have to get over my assumption about the Old Testament. For years I saw the first books of the bible as nothing more than an encyclopedia **Brute**-tanica containing God's hard unquestionable rules to be obeyed and stories of bad things happening to people who ignored those laws. I mean it even had a book called **Do**-teuronomy!

Before I had a cell phone or a computer, I began to dig into the Hebraic culture of my Jewish Messiah and His disciples. For thirty years, I felt like a six year old trying to clear the field of wrong thinking weeds with only a Strong's Concordance *hoe*. Once connected to the Infinity and Beyond of the Internet, I spent hours gleaning from those who have published the results of their own Hebraic studies.

One of them, W. H. Sanford, spent years in putting together the Messianic Aleph Tav Interlinear Scriptures. Mr. Sanford found over four hundred thousand Hebrew words that make up the thirty-nine books of the King James Bible with well over thirty thousand that are only used one time. Yet Strong's concordance only lists a little over eight thousand Hebrew words with a focus on the primary meaning of the basic Hebrew words. Hundreds of different Hebrew words share the exact same Strong's number because their primary root words are the same. Root words can be widely diverse in meaning but it would have been insane for Strong to list every unique word in his dictionary that is spelled a little differently with a different number, when all he needed to do was express the primary basic Hebrew words and root words, to convey their various meanings. (www.AlephTavScriptures.com)

That explains why one English word is used to translate different Hebrew words. For example, there are sixty verses containing the English word, *perfect*. Yet if those same sixty verses were looked up in an interlinear bible we would find fourteen Hebrew words where English translators went with *perfect* for all of them.

As much as I appreciate being able to use the Internet to search for answers to my many questions, I'm not so sure thanks are in order for the social media in confirming Ecclesiastes 12:12; opinions ready to be expressed are endless. Comments of an accusatory nature from *preachers* of diversity and tolerance are made as they attack those who disagree with their political or religious experienced opinion by labeling (libeling?) their dissenters as heretics.

Like their bible counterparts, Internet and TV Pharisees fear losing their cash crop if people start reading and adhering to the True Word of God.

The first century religious leaders went so far as to get the people stirred up by setting up **false** witnesses against Stephen. The perjurers said they heard him speak **against** the temple, the Torah (Teachings), that Jesus would destroy the temple and would transform the customs which Moses had given them. At least they took off their *prayer shawls* and threw them at Saul's feet for him to guard before throwing stones.

It's sort of funny that Saul would later become a believer in this very same Messiah Stephen gave witness then had to defend himself from the same **false** accusations Stephen faced; that he was teaching apostasy from Moses and not to walk in the customs of the Jewish fathers. (StT Acts 6:13; 7:58; Acts 21:20-21)

Saul, who was called Paul after his conversion, *defended* himself from the accusation of being a pest and causing strife for all Jewish people by confessing to believing everything established by the Teachings and written in the Prophets, and *he worshiped the God of his Jewish ancestors* **according to the Way.** (StT Acts 24:14)

The truth was Stephen and Paul were NOT teaching to abandon the principles of Moses and the customs of the Jewish fathers because they both *practiced* the **LORD's** appointed Sabbaths and Feasts. It was the tacked on rules of the traditions of men that they were putting out to pasture. (StT Leviticus 23:2)

If Paul thought Torah (our old testament) had been done away with, then exactly to what *"All Scripture"* was he referring in his second letter to Timothy? Considering Paul's letters were written before the first gospel, which was Mark's while Matthew, Luke's writing (which included Acts) then John's gospels were not recorded until later, that leaves *Torah* as the **All Scripture.**

This means *Torah* is God-inspired to use for teaching, reproof, restoration, for training in standing right with God so that true believers are equipped perfectly for every good work. Thanks to his grandmother Lois and mother Eunice for teaching him these *sacred writings* from his childhood, Timothy has the same sincere faith dwelling in him that had first dwelt in them. Torah makes wise for salvation through faith in Messiah Yeshua. (StT 2 Timothy 3:14-17)

Not all of us had a mother and grandmother who did not shirk their responsibility of establishing faith and Truth in and for their own posterity, as well as ours. That's why Peter wrote his second letter to wake anyone listening out of sleep to a pure way of thinking that is without mixture of meaning. It is up to us to exercise unbroken vigilance so that we do not depart from what God says is True by those untaught in Torah and distort His doctrine since they do not have a staff to lean on, the power of truth. We must continually increase in grace and in knowledge of our Lord and Savior. Like the hungry noble-minded Jewish Berean who were ready and willing to welcome Paul's message. All the same they vigorously examined up and down the Hebrew Scrolls to see if what he said was keeping with the Torah. Remember, the New Testament had not yet been written so the Bereans studied the Old Testament. (StT 2 Peter 3:1, 14-18; Proverbs 2:1-5; Acts 17:11)

As a diehard fan of the King James translation, I had a hard time admitting the "authorized version" label did not mean my beloved KJV was the only version that God recognizes nor was it the one Jesus and His disciples used.

Once I accepted that all English translations were not the original language Scriptures and subject to the translators' religious slant, it became a bit easier spotting its interpretation *weeds* as I continued to criss cross the rows (verses) to the the right (new testament) then back to the left (old testament) of my bible.

Granted, translating other languages into English had to be complicated, but I couldn't help but wonder if the King James mistranslations were intentionally done to plant seeds of enmity towards our first century ancestors in the Faith or just in ignorance of Hebrew idioms?

How did the pagan queen's celebration, Easter, get inserted for *pascha*, the Greek word for the Jewish Feast, *Passover*? (StT Acts 12:4)

Does anyone recognize these Hebrew guys: Hananiah, Mishael, and Azariah? We know them better as Shadrach, Meshach and Abednego; the names given them by the chief of the royal eunuchs when they were taken captive to Babylon. Since an individual's identity is tied up in his name, could the pagan name change be an attempt to erase their Hebraic connection and immerse them into the Babylonian mixture of worldly values and customs? I have no idea why the king didn't call these three by their Hebrew names as he continued to do so for Daniel instead of Belteshazzar, the Babylonian name given Daniel by his chief official.

The name, Esther, may have been used to hide Hadassah's Jewish identity for her to gain entrance in the Persian beauty contest so she would be in the right place at the right time. Not knowing Esther's Jewish heritage, Haman broke the hospitality rule where it was considered a terrible sin for anyone to accept hospitality from a host only to turn around and do something evil against them and their family.

Who knows whether our spiritual Jewish identity has been hidden for centuries only to be revealed after we take on the responsibility of royal priests in His Kingdom to give the portion of food (bring eternal accountability to all who hear) in the appointed time? (StT Luke 12:42)

As for *God* and *Jesus*, anyone feeling they have a definitive answer to *"What is His Name and what is His Son's Name, if you can tell?" (Proverbs 30:4)*

"God" can be used as a hollow cuss word or a generic name used by any religion. In written form, the Hebrews leave out the vowels whether it's the tetragrammaton YHWH for Yahweh or G-d. But what if that's a manmade tradition? I'm not looking to cull out any Christian traditions that God isn't pleased with only to replace them with Jewish ones that He feels the same about.

Strong's Concordance has the Hebrew *Yah* for the proper name of Israel's God and *Yhvh* (Yahweh) for LORD.

There is no "J" sound in Hebrew, so I doubt the angel told a Hebrew Mary to give her son the Greek name *"Jesus"*especially since that name has only been used in King James translations for around 400 years. In the 1611 King James Version of the Bible, His name was written as *Iesous*, the transliteration of *Yehoshua Yahweh;* the One who delivers or rescues.

Being in unfamiliar territory, I sought the lead of someone who knows the 'Hebraic custom' ropes. Turns out several Messianic Hebrew speakers differed on how to address our Father or His Son.

If the experts can't agree if "Jesus" is supposed to be called *Yeshua, Y'shua, Yahshua, Yehoshua,* or *Yahushua* then how am I supposed to get His Name right?

What I am convinced of, no matter what we call Him, we should not make the Name of the One and ONLY Unchanging One worthless by *saying* we have known Him but don't keep His commandments. We honor His Name by remaining in Him and walking the same walk just as His Son walked.

It has been pretty much settled that the first of the first century believers were Jewish so from where did the "Christian" label come? For a term that has stuck all these years, it surprisingly appears only three times in the New Testament. In Acts 11:26, it was non-believers who initially tagged Jesus' disciples this way but later in Acts 24:5, Paul's accuser, Tertullus, referred to Paul as of the *Nazarene* sect who observe the Teachings of Yahweh and couldn't tell them apart from "regular" Jews if it were not for the fact that they believed in the Messiah from Nazareth.

Agrippa may have been Jewish in his religion but he was devoted to the Roman Empire when he so-called *it* a Christian sect Paul almost had him believing enough to join.

Peter's take is no **follower of The Way** was to suffer as a murderer or a thief or evildoer but if they were *contemptuously* called a Christian, they should not be ashamed but give thanks to God for His good grace no matter the circumstance. (StT Acts 26:28; 1 Pet 4.16)

The "Christian" label didn't really adhere as a badge of honor until the second or third century. That was around the time a "church" started being the place for believers to go and just sit to hear one man talk instead of the two by two Jesus sent out. (StT Mark 6:7; Luke 10:1)

The word, church, is not found in the Bible. The congregation of believers was called *Ekklesia* and had a plurality of elders who oversaw the daily meetings at a synagog but mostly in different houses where **everybody** was able to use their spiritual gifting to strengthen the faith of each other. Undeterred by their difficulties, the yielded believers continued to share their *bread* (substance of Instructions which prompts a change afterwards) with intense joy and gladness. (StT 1 Corinthians 14:26; Acts 2:46)

As for the Hebrew idioms, like in English, they are an expression from the local culture and cannot be understood from the meanings of its separate words thereby should not be translated word for word, but thought for thought.

If a non-English speaking person only looked up the definition of each word in the idiom *"Party until the cows come home,"* I'm pretty sure they would never come up with the expression's correct meaning, "For a very long time."

As a foreigner to the Hebrew culture, I didn't get the drift that a person with an "evil eye" is a Hebrew idiom for someone who is greedy or stingy whereas a "good eye" means a generous person. (StT Proverbs 28:22; Matthew 6:22)

The Hebrew idioms *"destroy the law"* and *"fulfilling the law"* had my understanding of what Jesus said as one way but got really changed up after realizing the first means "misinterpreting Scripture" while the second means "correct interpretation."

> *"Do not think that I came to do away with, or **to bring an incorrect interpretation to**, the Torah or the Prophets. I did not come to do away with but to bring **spiritual** abundance, for the Torah (Teaching) to be obeyed as it should be and God's promises to receive fulfillment." (Matthew 5:17, **emphasis mine**)*

As much as I would love for Mr. Strong to have put together an exhaustive Hebrew to English cheat sheet, there's still plenty to be learned from using his concordance. Spiritual growth can happen by simply reading the King James or any Biblical translation but sometimes I wonder how many confessing believers are bible readers.

After someone had the gall to post politically incorrect Bible verses online, a few emphatic commenters asserted "MY God would NEVER say/do…!" Their sentences were finished with what they deemed too harsh or judgmental for a loving God. To them, God was tantamount to memory foam; comfortable and conforming into *their* image. By refusing to read or believe the scriptures, they wanted God to do things to their liking thereby fundamentally flipping the meaning of 1 John 4:17 where we are to be just like *Him* during our time in this world. If our lives are to reflect Jesus, then we need to read the front of the Book that doesn't just describe Him but IS Him.

Incredibly, I witnessed a woman who defiantly stuck to her *doctrinal* guns even after a scripture was read that was contrary to what she had always believed. Ignorance may be bliss, but being religiously **stupid**-fied is like jumping up and down for joy right over a cliff.

According to 1 Peter 4:17, the time has ended where God overlooks ignorance in His household. We need to change our old way of thinking, reject unenlightened assumptions and to seek God's purpose for our lives. This includes rethinking the "Good News" of the Christian recruiting gospel where all you need is to repeat a prayer for a secured entry through the pearly gates then *grace* lets you live life without rules.

I'm not implying the "repeat after me" pray-*er* wasn't sincere. My concern is whether or not they know the cost of the covenant requirements to being a Kingdom citizen. According to Jesus, if anyone wanted to build a tower so the farmers of the vineyard could keep watch, they should first calculate the expense to prevent being a laughingstock by not being able to finish once the construction started. (StT Luke 14:28-33)

Yet it seems the only "costs" a *prayer repeater* needs to concern himself with is the option of playing the Christian Lotto (the tithe) during collection times.

It's funny that some who preach the Old Testament has been done away with are the biggest Malachi 3:10 pushers. Except the biblical tithe wasn't done the way they would have you think. There is a small quantity of crops (first fruits), to be given to the priests who were not given a salary or land inheritance described in Deuteronomy 8:1-11. After that small tithe is given, Deuteronomy 26:12 states that the year of tithing is in the third year and is to be given to the Levite priests, the new-comer with no inherited rights, the fatherless, and the widow, *so they may eat* within their gates and be filled. The tithe was never meant to line the pockets of preachers, support their opulent lifestyles or build grandiose church buildings while their own "partners" can't afford food or decent housing.

It's hard to tone down the rhetoric when we have an enemy who doesn't want his covert operation to be exposed. He's more than happy to keep us blissfully ignorant so he can twist Jesus' words, "It is written…" to his advantage. He knows most of us won't bother to learn the original meaning of God's spoken Word so he can get a *friendly* conversation meant to sharpen each other's minds, like iron sharpening iron, to become heated.

It's not usually the good sparks flying when the topic of grace vs works comes up between opposing attitudes. Especially when neither side realize Paul and James were not contradicting each other but were writing to different cultural groups.

Paul knew how to speak to the crowds who thought new converts had to adhere to strict *doctrinal* rules instead of being rooted in the Truth of Torah. Before his conversion, he had used tacked on doctrinal rules himself to excuse his own "search and destroy mission" of any who were of the Way. (StT Acts 9:1-2)

Deuteronomy 30:14 would be the very word of faith Paul openly proclaimed in Romans 10:5-8 where Moses wrote of the righteousness that is from the Torah. So Torah is the Word in our mouth and heart so we can *do* it.

Jesus paid the price for our Kingdom citizenship so there's nothing we can *do* to earn our own salvation. However, like living on a farm where everyone has a part to do for the good of the whole family, there are *actions* we have been created in Messiah Jesus to *do* as productive citizens of His Kingdom.

On the other hand, James had some folks implanting themselves at Torah's Table happily being fed and just a talkin' and a sittin' on their grace seed instead of gettin' out in the field and humbly plantin' a spiritual fruit crop. (StT Ephesians 2:8-10; James 2:17-22-26; 3:13.)

By reducing our truth perspective to a theological debate on any issue, the *Chief Instigator* can keep us overgrazing in the same old pasture of mistaken beliefs until we resign ourselves to drinking lifeless stagnated water from the leaky cisterns of our own making.

Why would anyone choose to swallow man-made-pond-scum edicts when they could move to another field and drink their fill from the Fountain of Living Waters?

We have to first experience the joy of drawing water out of the wells of *Yeshuah* (Hebrew Word for salvation or saving health), before we can express His Covenant loyalty towards others. Drinking in the rushing refreshment that is His Voice makes happy the **merciful,** those who act consistently with the revelation of God's covenant, and they will be shown **mercy.** (StT Ezekiel 43:2; Revelation 1:15; Jeremiah 2:13; 1 Corinthians 2:16; Zechariah 9:11; Isaiah 12:3; and Matthew 5:7)

By making covenant with Him, we are adopted into God's Spiritual family and treated as heirs to the family fortune. Please don't misunderstand. I am not advocating for present day Judaism that honors man made traditions over the pure unadulterated Torah.

*"He (The LORD) will **magnify** the Torah (Teaching) and make it honorable. But this is a people robbed and plundered. They are all of them snared in holes, and they are hidden in prison houses. They are for a prey and no one delivers, for a spoil, but no one is saying, **Restore!** Who among you will give ear to this? Who will listen and obey and hear for the time to come?"*

*Who gave Jacob for plunder and Israel to the robbers? Did not the LORD, He against whom we have sinned? **For they would not walk in His Ways, neither were they obedient to His Torah (Teaching)."** (Isaiah 42:22-24, **emphasis mine**)*

There is a big difference in the loving teachings of the Torah and the burdensome tacked on dogma commandments of religion that were not in the *original* Torah (Teachings).

Like never before there is a necessity of gatekeepers with the task of being constantly on the alert for any enemy advancing toward our land and will not hesitate to sound the warning for his fellow kingdom citizens. (StT Matthew 7:15; Mark 13:34; Ezekiel 33:3-7)

I don't want to grieve God from choosing me as a gatekeeper by turning back from following Him and give a half-hearted performance of His commandments similar to King Saul.

It all happened when it was God's time of vengeance upon Amalek for assaulting Israel on their way up from Egypt. Samuel gave King Saul the LORD's "search and destroy mission" of all that belonged to Amalek. To spare no one not even the cows, sheep, camels and donkeys.

King Saul struck the Amalekites but he and his men had a better idea. They would keep the best of the cows and sheep instead of udderly destroying them along with the vile and refuse.

The LORD tells on King Saul to Samuel. When King Saul sees Samuel coming he greets him with a blessing followed by telling Samuel he performed the LORD's command. Samuel comes back with if that was so, then why does he hear cattle mooing and sheep bleating? In his defense King Saul answered that he did do everything like God said with the slight variation of sparing the best to sacrifice to *Samuel's* God.

Samuel reminded King Saul he had one job to do; put an end to the existence of the Amalekites. So why did he give only partial obedience?

King Saul reiterated, that he obeyed the voice of the LORD and may have spared King Agag, but the cows and sheep were for sacrificing to the LORD *Samuel's* God.

Samuel wasn't haven't any of it and pointed out to King Saul that obeying the LORD's commands completely is better than offering sacrifices and listening out of a whole hearted love to Him is greater than all burnt offerings. (StT Deuteronomy 32:34; 1 Samuel 15:1-23; Mark 12:33)

King Saul's referencing God as *Samuel's* LORD reveals he did not personally have an intimate relationship with the LORD. Maybe that's why he felt free to be selective in his obedience.

Any other gatekeepers hear the mooing of Deception's Sacred Cows that have been left in our land to sully the refreshing Life Giving Water and steal spiritual nutrients away from the tender family herd? Are you willing to join me at this opportune time for a "search and destroy mission" to cull them? If so, then let's head 'em up, move 'em on, and cut 'em out!

Stirring the Golden Prayer Pot

Our Father, Your Name must always be honored as Holy!

Above everything else, I inquire to get to the bottom of what is approved of in Your eyes. By digging up the Truth covered by the dirt of man-made traditions, similar to harvesting the underground peanuts, I have gained a better understanding and reverence for You. So I mean no disrespect with all my questions but each new answer only whets my appetite for more of the whole Truth and nothing but Your Truth.

I want Your sharpened precepts to penetrate my heart so You have something to draw out of my inner being to give to the hungry and the afflicted. May they taste (relish intellectually) how good You are and find how happy are the ones who take refuge in You!

As I strain to listen to Your Answers over the clamor of the heresy surging herds, guide me continually in true knowledge and insight so my soul is satisfied through droughts like a field with a deep well that does not dry up.

With rejoicing and singing I will report for duty as a gatekeeper of Your House every morning making sure nothing You consider unclean will enter.

*Eventually You, the true Farmer, will judge at harvest time everything that I do according to my heart's hidden intent, whether it's good or evil. May Your Son find **the** faith in me when He returns.*

First Serving: Welcome Y'all!

'This One welcomes sinners and He eats with them.' ...When he finds [the one lost sheep] he places it upon his shoulders rejoicing.

(Luke 15:2 & 5)

Jesus/Yeshua is The Way, The Truth, and The Life. No one comes to the Father except through Him.

(StT John 14:6)

Why are so many people in a stew? This English idiom seems to be the gist of Psalm 2:1 asking *what* is goading people to embrace anger and chaos?

The irritating 'what' differs from one person to the next. It could be the catchy opinionated sound bites used by political rabble-rousers with personal agendas that send their devotees on a rampage. Or just the hassles of daily life.

To me, the biggest culprit is a depressing god-less worldview that is causing anxious folks to stave off their spiritual hunger pangs with quick-fix religious horse d'oovers instead of ending their inner peace famine by covenanting with The True Bread of Life.

Modern thought views time with a beginning that flat lines all the way to the end instead of a circular view of the ancient Hebrews of the Bible. Going around in circles could account for history seemingly repeating itself.

It's like Jesus took a story out of our recent headlines when He spoke of a current event about eighteen people killed in a tower accident. He used the tragedy to awaken His listeners' memories of the Teachings to walk the path exactly as Yahweh their Elohim had commanded so that they would thrive and live long in the land of their inheritance. It wasn't that the folks who died were bad people who deserved an untimely death but accidents do happen so people needed to be more concerned about their long term (as in *forever*) living arrangements than if the tower had targeted only sinful people.

Even today, we are to **follow the whole instruction** [Way] the Lord God has **commanded** [Truth] so that we may **live** [Life]. Jesus is the **Way,** the **Truth,** and the **Life;** to see the Father we have to perceive the Son. As the Living Word, His recorded Voice are signposts pointing the Way back to His Kingdom's original set up in Eden's Garden. This enclosed garden is where our Lord God fenced off a separate plot of ground for man's home and planted top-quality trees and herbs fit for a king there. (StT Deuteronomy 5:29-33; Luke 13:3-5; John 14:6)

With so many saying they don't need to read the Book about Jesus to believe in Him, it seems God is having to duplicate His hunger test with us in the same way He did with Ancient Israel in order to teach by personal experience that man does not live by bread only. Just like ancient Israel, all we have to do is humbly *keep and live* our lives according to God's Instructions but, just like them, we collectively need to be knocked off our *self-reliant high horse*.

Or am I the only one with God as a personal Tour Guide on a 'forty year' *scenic route* to learn what is in my heart; whether or not I will keep His Teachings?

A famine in the land is the backdrop for several Bible stories where the collective starved spiritual condition of a nation caused God to *suddenly* dispatch non-professional prophets for drought explaining duties. One reluctant pop up prophet, Amos, gives the impression he was minding his own business back on the farm raising cattle when God tapped him for the task of telling the people the famine won't be food or water, **but God's Word.**

Amos was sent to folks acting similar to the ones Jeremiah (6:16) spoke God's message about standing by the roads and looking for the *ancient path*. By **walking on this path**, they would find rest for their souls.

Even way back then, there were people who thought His rules for guiding their thoughts and behavior simply didn't apply to them. Wanting to keep the soft, fluffy, feel good, twisted lies of their traditions, they felt justified in rejecting God's Truth tellers for teachers who confirmed their erroneous beliefs. They seemed to have cared less if any one would be serving an Original Recipe Truth Happy Meal so God had to take the attention getting detail up a notch. This time, it is a double whammy famine for God's Word *and* food that we can find in progress in 2 Kings 4:38-41.

Some sort of safety labeling might have come in handy for the one picking herbs in a field when Prophet Elisha tells his servant to boil a stew in the large pot for the rest of the prophets. Not recognizing a certain vine didn't stop the young *prophet in training* from gathering its wild gourds to cut up and use. While eating some of the pot-luck stew, the men ran out of luck and had to stop eating because there was *death* in the pot.

The Hebrew word used in this passage for field, *sadeh*, has the meaning of being unenclosed. Without being protected by a fence, the field in this story was open to uncultivated plants with wild gourds that can cause severe cramps when eaten in small portions but death in larger.

This particular *cull*-inarian lacked familiarity with true life fruit and mistakenly picked its diarrhea causing false look alike. The loose interpretations of God's Teachings served up by Israel's spiritual leaders had caused the world to go to pot. They weren't just teaching tolerance for the locals' religions, but were feeding the people a spiritual death stew of religious and hybrid humanistic beliefs picked from the open pasture of false cults.

If Elisha and his students had been able to drop by grandma's kitchen, she would've cooked them some of her garden fresh okra, potatoes, and corn. (Oh how I regret all those wasted good okra eatin' years because of my stubborn refusal to believe the itchy fuzzy pods could taste good when fried.)

It wasn't just at supper time that every visitor to my grandparents' home was greeted with an offer of the most comfortable place to sit, something to eat, and a *pop* to drink. Their guests were never made to feel awkward by being ignored or left alone.

From the field data of living in seven towns divided between four states since my marriage in 1975, I have surmised grandma's old fashioned food friendliness is almost nonexistent. Is hospitality, like my accent, just an Oklahoma thang?

After one of those moves, Scott was still at work when I answered a stranger's knock at the door. My visitor identified himself as a member of a local church so I reckoned it was okay to ask him in. The expression on his face seemed he was just as shocked as I was to hear my enthusiastic welcome, "My husband's *not* home. Come on in!"

Not exactly how I meant to convey my concern of being alone with a man if I obeyed my grandma and Hebrews 13:2 that we should extend hospitality to everyone; even to people we don't know. It was a relief that the church guy declined my embarrassing invitation and a good thing for him that we weren't living in the Bible times when the very lives of the nomadic people depended on the hospitality of strangers.

If any of these nomads departed from the well-worn path that led to one fresh pasture with a good watering hole to the next, they could become lost and wander around without a sense of direction.

These ancient travelers didn't have roadside *Desert Inns* to lodge overnight, nor any fast food *Brisket Kings* to quench a thirst or satisfy hunger pangs in what could be a hostile environment. In some towns there were *pandocheion,* the Greek word translated *inn* for the pay to stay public house. It's where the Good Samaritan (the despised outcast because of his mixed race and compromised religion) offered hospitality to the injured stranger. (StT Luke 10:34)

This is not the same Greek word for the *inn* that was full when Joseph and Mary arrived in Bethlehem. That would be *kataluma,* the guest-chamber on the upper floor of an Ancient Eastern dwelling; the same word translated "upper room" where Jesus and His twelve had supper. (StT Luke 22:11)

Because of Joseph's lineage, there's a good chance the family dwelling where Jesus was born was the very one that belonged to Boaz and Ruth. If the guest room was full, Mary would've been given privacy in the lower room where the family's animals were brought in at night with the stone ledge feeding trough (manger) located near the door.

Joseph would briefly welcome his unexpected but special guests there. It wasn't random field hands who arrived after being serenaded by an angel choir. Nope. They were Levitical shepherds who were the only ones with the 'right stuff' to guard the destined-to-be sacrificed-Passover lambs. Following religious protocol, they examined all newborn lambs for spot or blemishes then swaddled all the flawless ones. This elite task force continued to guard these special lambs in temple owned pastures in Bethlehem during the year before Passover. Only this angel choir could convince these passionate shepherds to leave their guard posts.

After witnessing a *swaddled* Jesus lying on the stone threshold manger as the prophetic sign to lying swaddled on the stone after his death, these special shepherds returned to their holy assignment glorifying God over all the amazing things they heard and saw.

Jesus wouldn't have been given The Name the angel had called Him *(Yeshua)* when appearing to Mary until He was circumcised on His eighth day.

When the days of Mary's *"purification were completed according to the Torah (Teaching) of Moses, they brought Him up to **Jerusalem** to present Him to the Lord, just as it has been written in the Torah (Teaching) of the Lord that "Every male opening the womb will be called holy to the Lord," (Exodus 13:2) and to give an offering according to that which was said in the Torah (Teaching) of the Lord, "A pair of turtledoves, or two young doves." (Luke 2:8-24, **emphasis mine**)*

The time table for the days of purification set in Leviticus 12:3-4 is a seven day period and a 33 day period for a total of 40 days. Jesus would've been around a month old when Joseph and Mary left *Bethlehem* to go to *Jerusalem.*

According to the Torah, if a person couldn't afford a lamb, then he must bring two doves or two young pigeons as an offering. (StT Leviticus 5:7) Joseph and Mary's offering makes me believe they hadn't hosted the Wise men yet. By bringing a poor man's offering, they could not have already possessed the wealth given by the magi.

The Bible lists three kinds of gifts but does not disclose the entire wealth given nor the amount of men needed to protect it as they traveled the dangerous distance, similar to when a great *train* accompanied the Queen of Sheba when she came to meet King Solomon. (StT 1 Kings 10:2, 10)

The Hebrew word for train, *chayil*, is the same word interpreted 'virtuous' in Proverbs 31:10 describing the warrior bride. A band of war worthy men and/or women is just the protection you need if your camels are laden with expensive gifts for a king.

Who were the non-Hebrew Magi watching for the sign of the Jewish King's coming anyway? I'm glad you asked.

The Greek, *Magos*, is the name given by the Babylonians (Chaldeans), Medes, Persians, and others, to the wise men, priests, physicians, astrologers, interpreters of dreams, etc. I propose they are connected with the chief officials of Babylonia, called *Rab-Mag* in Hebrew. The same sort of magi in Daniel chapter 2 where the king sent for his usual advisors to come interpret the troubling dream he couldn't even remember.

Disregarding the Chaldean wise men protests that no one on earth is able to do what he demanded, the king ordered all the wise men of Babylon to be put to death. Since this included Daniel and his friends, Daniel puts in his bid for more time during which God compassionately gave him the secret of the dream.

Before giving the interpretation, Daniel refused the gifts the king offered just to make it clear he was not doing it for money. But later, he accepted the grateful king's gifts along with a promotion of being ruler and head over all the wise men of Babylon.

I suggest that all the wise men, who owed their lives to Daniel, would be very appreciative and eager to learn about his God who had given him their life saving dream interpretation.

Daniel's ability to reproduce in his flesh may have been cut off when he was made a eunuch, but I propose Daniel was able to leave something for posterity through his revelations to his grateful students. Perhaps Daniel's wealth had been stored up along with his instructions to be passed on to the next crop of wise men to keep a lookout for the star of the One Who was to be born King of the Jewish people. When the sign finally appeared, the magi knew it was time to load up the camels with treasures for *the* King.

Could all this be another of all the intricate details around Jesus' life left unrecorded? Or is this the caravan of camels bringing gold and frankincense that Isaiah saw? (StT Isaiah 60:6)

Matthew 2:11 states these men came into the **house** when they saw the **child** with His mother. I have no idea if the family had returned to

Bethlehem after they offered their sacrifice but some time has transpired because the Greek word for child, *paidion,* implies a child in training possibly as old as seven years. No matter how old Jesus actually was, we can all calculate that it probably took at least a couple of years due to the distance and the slow travel of men walking beside heavy laden camels.

The Bible doesn't record if Joseph personally hosted all these men. Without hotels to check into, a traveler would wait by a well or the city gate in hopes someone locally would offer him a drink of water and a place to stay. Once inside his host's home, the guest would be supplied water to wash his feet, served a meal, and his animals tended. Protection was provided for a visitor even at the cost of the host's own life and/or the lives of his family.

Simon lapsed in fulfilling his host duties by failing to give foot washing water to Jesus after He entered his house.

When Lot invited God's two messengers to stay at his house, he was obliged to keep his guests safe from the demands of the men of Sodom by offering his virgin daughters to be molested. (StT Luke 7:44; Genesis 19:8)

My country girl mindset still has a hard time grasping the ancient hospitality's shelter protocol of protecting guests at the cost of the host's own life and/or the lives of his family. I mean, in that ancient culture the person or persons you take in for a night or two could be total strangers one minute, but they become "friends" as long as they are your guests. This gets me that Jesus said that there's not a stronger commitment than to lay down your life for a *friend* (someone with whom you are in covenant).

Jesus told His disciples to accept a hospitality offer from a trustworthy person then bless their host home with peace if their host also welcomed their Kingdom power message. He went on to say that whoever welcomes a prophet gets a share of a prophet's reward and the same went for welcoming someone who observes and practices Torah. No one will lose his reward if he gives one of His humble followers a drink of water simply for the fact they belong to Jesus. This hospitality drink oblation is pretty important for anyone wanting to hang on to his reward. When Jesus returns, He will cull the go-off-in-their-own-direction inhospitable goats from the truth-following-hospitable sheep.

If anyone ignored His disciples by giving the double cold shoulder of refusing to offer "Hospitality 101" *plus* not listening to the Lord's message they carried, His taught ones were to leave that place taking their peace with them. Jesus said that the **ancient pits of inhospitality,** Sodom and Gomorrah, would fare better on judgment day than the townspeople who ignored His disciples and refused to listen to the prophetic Word.

(StT Matthew 10:5-15, 40-42; Mark 9:41; Matthew 25:31-46)

With all the notions for the destruction of Sodom and Gomorrah, who would've thought their lack of hospitality was a big part of it? Just to be on the safe side, I started repenting of any missed hospitality opportunities. Among others, I wondered if this one in 1995 fell into that category.

My sister Kay had asked me to help with her idea of a book to organize favorite or clipped recipes. Customers could potentially create a treasured heirloom for future generations to enjoy the unique flavor of their ancestry simply by filling *The Farmhouse Collection* pages with their family's secret recipes.

Of course we had to include a few farm themed recipes of our own like *Homestead Rolls* and *Oklahoma Cow Patties* (Chocolate No-Bake Cookies). An untested garlic bean recipe was added to the printed collection as *Skunk Beans*. After preparing them for her family, Kay discovered the beans were befitting their new name; they stunk in smell and taste.

A trade show for a televised home shopping network gave us the opportunity to showcase our recipe collection. Being 4-H Club demonstration alumni and the first to arrive, Kay and I were undaunted by the large open room filled with 400 empty tables. As the room filled with the other entrepreneurs, we noticed that all of them were keeping the two chairs at each table for themselves. We had assumed the chairs were for the judges.

Instead of swapping our display's orientation to match the rest of the herd, I wish we had remembered our raisin' and thought to bring a sample of the *Oklahoma Cow Patties* to offer the judges along with our chairs. It might not have swayed them from their decision not to select our book for the show, but possibly we would've given them the feeling they were glad they stopped by.

Oh well, at least the predicament about the 'stinker' recipe included in the already printed books was simplified. As each book was sold, we would cross out the *Skunk Beans* recipe with a black permanent marker

"X" then write, "These Stink!" Some people thought it was intentionally done for humor on our part. Okay, we'll go with that.

Of course the Bible is the real treasured heirloom collection where the Lord tells His secrets to and makes friends through covenant with those who honor Him. The *ancient* Hebrew family foibles were written and passed down so we could learn from their *recipes for disaster* so as to not cook up any of our own. (StT Psalm 25:14; 1 Corinthians 10:11)

We can't take a permanent marker "X" to the *Skunk Beans'* biographies of the liars, cowards, drunkards, adulterers, murderers, etc, recorded in scripture because most of those stinkers are considered the *Heroes of Faith*. This list of people, who made lamentable life choices, gives well-grounded hope that no matter what our stories all of us have a chance of being inducted into *The Faith Hall of Fame* too. We just need to believe, like they did, that God can and will do the impossible in our situation. (StT Hebrews 11; Luke 18:27)

Getting caught up in the "everyone's doing it so they must be right" mentality caused Kay and I to switch from being the lone-renegade-table-setter-upper in that large trade show room. Yet, the flood, the twelve spies, and the Golden Calf stories sort of substantiate that the ignorance or indifference of the herd cannot change Truth. (StT Genesis 7:1; Numbers 12; Exodus 31:32)

It turns out Noah's carpentry skills were better than his preaching since the only converts that were saved after all those years building the ark were his family of eight.

Guess the majority should have clipped and saved the two good reports while discarding the ten spies' fearful ones if they ever wanted to whip up any recipes from some of that "flowing milk and honey" available in their God Promised Land. But the Hebrews fear and unbelief got them forty years of *desert* instead of *dessert*.

There is a tendency to get caught up in the Golden Calf herd mentality if we fear being wrong, ostracized or ridiculed. Sacred Cow worship will continue if we don't get God's opinion on any interpretation based solely on the premise it is a widely held standard issue belief.

In 1 Kings 13, a young prophet paid the ultimate price to learn he shouldn't put his trust in the words of a man, even if that man claimed to be speaking for God. This particular pop up prophet comes on the scene because God was not pleased with the culture gratifying religious ceremonies set up in disobedience to His covenant requirements.

King Jeroboam had nullified any covenant guarantees when he attempted to clinch the people's votes by changing the day of worship and placing a "church" on every corner so the citizens didn't have to travel to the one and only God's house in Jerusalem. The king's more conveniently located opulent cultic worship temples were resplendent with golden calves and priests whose ancestry were not of Levi's, the only legit bloodline that God said could be priests. (StT 1 Kings 12)

Prophet No-Name gives the politically incorrect message that God was sending someone to do some House cleaning. Like a lot of people when someone points out they are wrong, King Jeroboam is ticked. Jeroboam's hand shriveled up when he ordered Prophet Nonconformist to be seized. Recognizing the symbolism of his power drying up, Jeroboam cries out for the man of the True God to pray for his hand to return to normal.

The prophet does. The king's hand was.

As a reward, the king invites the True God prophet to his house for refreshments. The young prophet answers that God's instructions were clear for while he was there; he was not to eat a snack, drink water or even travel back the same way he came. Yet, for some reason the young prophet lingers in the neighborhood instead of swiftly getting out of Dodge.

There was a local old prophet who heard the news of what all happened at the palace and went looking for the young prophet in order to extend his own hospitality. God's young prophet basically said the same thing he had already told the king; that he couldn't eat or drink with him either because God said so.

The young prophet should not have trusted the old prophet because he lied that he had been visited by an angel with the message that he was to escort the young prophet to his house to feed him bread and water. While they were sitting at the old prophet's table, God spoke a **true** message through the **lying** old prophet. Because the young prophet strayed from God's strict instructions and did not honor the command of his True God when he ate the bread and water (making covenant) in the place He said not to, the young man was going to die.

The young prophet flunked God's test to see if he would walk after

Him, keep *His commandments*, obey *His Voice* and serve *Him only*. On his way out of town, the young man was killed by a lion but his donkey was not.

Based on God's own words that a prophet who entices His people off the path He commanded them to follow should be put to death in order to expel the evil from the community, it doesn't seem fair that God didn't send the lion to tear to pieces the lying old prophet. (StT Deuteronomy 13:3-7)

The death penalty may have been meant as a strong deterrent against *false* "Thus saith the Lord" declarations, but it seems to be directed more towards those enticing God's people to go, *in His Words*, whoring after other husbands.

When God entered into a marriage covenant with the Hebrew slaves the day He brought them out of Egypt, He became *Ishi* which means *husband*.

Ba'al, the common name for these other gods, also has a meaning of a *husband*.

In English, the word *husband* looks to mean the same for God and the no-god but in the original language *Ishi and ba'al* have drastically different meanings in how they treat their wives.

Ishi refers to how God regards His beloved with tender affection and allows her freedom whereas *ba'al* is used in the sense of how a stern taskmaster uses domination and hierarchy to make his *possession* fearfully submit.

Once we can hear God's loving tone of Voice in His Ten Vows (Commandments), we can understand how a loving God reacts after placing His *Wings* over Israel, only to see them going after and speaking lovingly about other gods. It can be liken to one of a husband catching his wife on the phone or in bed with another man. (StT Hosea 2:16-2; Exodus 20:5; 34:14)

Oh how much easier it would be to understand God's covenants (Noahic, Abrahamic, Mosaic, David's or even the wedding one), if the details were spelled out. Maybe the original Bible writers didn't feel the need to waste ink and scroll paper describing things their Hebrew readers would have already been familiar. Which is different from anyone purposely manipulating the meat of God's Word in order to deceive. (StT Galatians 1:8)

Deception was not the basis of the story about a daughter who asked her mom why she cut off both ends of the piece of meat before cooking it. Her mom said it was because that's how her mom had always done it. When asked, the grandmother also said she was only doing it the way her mom had. Thankfully, the great-grandmother was still around to solve the mystery of how the unusual culinary tradition began; because it was the only way the meat would fit in her pot.

Silly traditions have been followed for generations just because no-one ever thought to question the narrative about why they practiced what they do.

For the longest, it never occurred to me to ask for the original recipe of making *disciples* even though Jesus told us to go make some. (StT Matthew 28:19)

Turns out that the Hebrew recipe for making a disciple, *talmid,* is a bit more involved than simply making an instant *cup o' convert.* Training in Truth takes time and is more involved than stirring up pop quizzes so whoever might be following you around could gain mere head knowledge.

A disciple wannabe would leave his family to spend years closely watching the master rabbi live life. Only after he became to be of the same character as his master through actual lifestyle practice could he pass on his rabbi's lifestyle teachings to his own *talmidim.* Paul was speaking in 1 Corinthians 11:1 about this kind of rabbi/*talmid* relationship when he said to follow him as he follows Messiah.

To be handpicked by a highly sought out rabbi was reaffirming to the disciple since a popular rabbi only chose those they thought had the potential and/or commitment to become who he is. Paul bragged on being a *talmid* of Gamaliel. (StT Acts 22:3)

Rabbis used a method of teaching which was to ask questions to be answered with a question in order to expand his *talmidim's* understanding. (StT Proverbs 1:7)

As a rabbi, Jesus employed the rabbinic questioning technique along with *remez,* which hints at a deeper meaning treasure just below the surface by leaving something off of what is spoken. He quoted a portion of scripture then let His listeners, who knew the Torah, fill in the blanks. I guess this means my guess earlier was correct; the Hebrew authors could assume their fellow Hebrew readers would possess an extensive knowledge of Scripture so they could be brief in conveying a great deal of information.

Jesus turning over Temple tables, healing the blind and lame didn't seem to get the high priest and the Torah teachers fired up as much as the children singing and they wondered if Jesus was deaf. That's when Jesus did the *remez* thing by partially quoting Psalm 8:2. After asking if they had never read "children and babies sing His praise," He then left off the rest of that Psalm that gave the reason the children were singing; to silence **His enemies and all who oppose Him**. The self-righteous religious leaders became indignant knowing Jesus was talking about them. (StT Matthew 21:15)

The more of those "cut off end pieces" of His Word I find, the more I understand why John said every detail of Jesus' life was not recorded because the world's pot couldn't hold all the books that would be needed. (StT John 21:25)

Missing information isn't the only problem we have to deal with while attempting to correctly understand what the bible transcribers meant. There's a few extra "ingredients" added centuries after the "original recipe" was written.

The verses about the woman caught in adultery make for some great sermon illustrations to prove none of us are without sin so we shouldn't be quick to throw condemnation stones at others. Yet, that story was added in the fifth century and not in John's original manuscript where surely he, a Torah observant follower of Yeshua/Jesus, would have noted *both* the man and woman *caught in the act* were to be stoned. (StT Leviticus 20:10; Deuteronomy 22:22)

After all, adultery works both ways.

In Judaism, adultery was a sin against God, so both participants were to be stoned where the practice of other societies was to punish the woman only. Those non-Hebrew groups viewed her as a possession of the husband, so her crime was not a moral one but concerned the husband's *property* rights and he could punish her how he wished.

I'm not meaning to place condemnation on any reader who might have missed the mark in this way. If we refuse to admit we have ALL sinned we are only deluding ourselves and His Word is not in us. We are considered righteous if we've gotten back on God's established path to His pasture and Living Water NOT if we get all religious. (StT Genesis 39:9; Proverbs 6:29; John 1:8)

Bringing up this story of the woman caught in adultery was just my way of showing how a false doctrine can get passed off as truth. One modern translation footnoted this story by admitting it was not found in the older manuscripts, but it *sounds* like Jesus so they accepted it as authentic, and felt it would be unfortunate to omit it. As much as I still love to read this translation, I disagree with the translators for this version who admittedly recognize that John 7:53 to 8:11 are not included in the original manuscripts, but it "feels" like *their* idea of *Jesus*, so they'll keep it in there where readers will believe this story actually occurred.

Isn't that how sacred cows are interbred with the pure Truth bloodline? If something sounds and feels good then it must be true so let's slap the Name of Jesus on it to make it exempt from criticism or questioning.

Technically, this was the very thing done with the *fiery serpent* God had commanded Moses to set up for the people's deliverance. The Hebrews had become discouraged because of the Way and murmured against God, Who then responded by sending fiery serpents among the people. A few bites later many people had died and the others had started confessing their sin of speaking against the LORD. The LORD told Moses to make an image of a serpent and set it upon a pole so the bitten repentant can look up and live. (StT Numbers 21:4-9)

Fast forward to when Hezekiah begins to reign by doing what was *right* in the sight of LORD. What exactly would that "right" be?

> "He removed the high places and broke the images and cut down the groves and **broke in pieces the brazen serpent** that Moses had made, **for until those days the children of Israel burn incense to it.**" (2 Kings 18:3-4, **emphasis mine**)

The serpent on the pole may have been God appointed for a specific time and purpose but the people sinned by keeping it around and worshiping *it* instead of the Healer.

When Jesus was explaining to Nicodemus about his necessity to be born from above, He pointed out that in the same way as Moses lifted the serpent up in the wilderness so also it was necessary for Him to be lifted up. **For this is the way** God loved the world. (StT John 3:3-17)

By keeping images of Jesus *still on a cross,* are we as guilty as the

Hebrews who worshiped the brazen serpent? Are we unknowingly holding Jesus up to public disgrace by becoming stagnant at the cross instead of maturing in the faith by feasting on the full measure of God's Word and experiencing the power of His Spirit? Or worse, if we choose to depart from the established Way it is impossible to be restored through repentance because that would be treating His sacrifice with contempt by crucifying Him anew for ourselves. (StT Hebrews 6:4-6)

What about Paul knowing only Jesus Messiah and Him crucified? According to his custom, he went to the synagogue of the Jewish people and spoke to them from the Torah Scrolls to explain the truth *"that it was necessary for the Messiah to suffer **and to be raised from the dead** and that 'The Messiah is this Y'shua' Whom I am proclaiming to you." (Acts 17:2-3, **emphasis mine**)*

Paul put the matter of the Messiah's death, being buried then rising on the third day according to the Scriptures in a nutshell by simply writing "Christ crucified." We are made righteous through faith in Messiah and knowing Him and the power of His resurrection, not from legalism. Those *dogmas* were nailed to the crucifixion tree. (StT 1 Corinthians 1:23, 2:21, 15:3-4; Philippians 3:10)

The teaching of many False Messiahs and Prophets that sinners can come as they are and get to stay that way because God's loving covenant is no longer relevant has deceived even some of God's handpicked ones.

The True Messiah welcomes repentant sinners to have a covenant meal so they can be changed into "friends" but He ignores the non-repentant. If you remember, Jesus refused to answer the scorning proud thief on the crucifixion tree with Him but gave grace to the humbled one. (StT Proverbs 3:34; James 4:6; 1 Peter 5:5)

Neither did the non-repentant get covered by, "Father, forgive them for they do not know what they are doing." That prayer is one Sacred Cow even I didn't want to touch, but I would be remiss if I didn't share that Luke 23:34 was not in some of the surviving original manuscripts but added in the fifth century.

The parable about a forgiving father playing host by welcoming home his repentant son is widely known as *The Prodigal Son*. For those not familiar with this story, it sort of goes like this:

Once there was a farmer who had two sons. One day the younger son came to his father and said, "Dad, I don't want to have to wait until you die to inherit my share of your estate. I want you to give me my share now."

So the father divided his property equally between the undemanding older son and the importunate younger. It didn't take long before the younger son set off to see the world.

The world's enticements quickly relieved the undisciplined son of all his money just as a drought caused an economic depression. Hired by a farmer to work the fields, the whippersnapper was so miserably hungry that the pigs' slop looked appetizing but no one offered him even their table scraps.

He finally came to his senses and thought, "All my father's farmhands have plenty of food. Why should I stay here and starve to death? I'll go home and apologize for doing wrong to God and my dad. I'll say 'I don't deserve to be called your son, but will you take me on to be your hired hand?'"

While the remorseful son was still a distance away, his dad had already spotted him and was on the move running towards him. Before the humbled young man could get out his beautifully prepared speech, his dad was hugging and kissing him then calling to the hired hands to quickly get the royal robes, shoes, and the family ring to royally dress him. Then he told them to prepare a supper of the best grass fed cow. It was to be a celebration feast for the son that was almost dead but now he's fully alive!

How was it that the dad just happened to see his son a *fur* piece away the day of his return? The ancient hospitality custom basically had the understanding it just wasn't right to eat alone. So the host father would stand at the door in hopes to share a meal with a stranger.

Once his invitation is accepted, the Head of the House has the responsibility of being host by attentively attending to his guests needs before they even have to ask. Matthew 6:8 and Psalm 139:2-4 has God in the role of LORD of *Hosts* by stating He knows what we need before we pray, our sitting down and getting up, our thoughts, our walking and lying down, well, He's just intimately acquainted with all our ways.

It is also the host father's duty to make his guests feel at home by making mealtime a mirthful experience. Mirth is more than just being cheerful, it implies noisy joy. It's being happy out loud!!

Joy breaks out *in the presence* of God's angels over even one sinner who changes his way of life. The Merry-Maker dances **before** (in front of) the angels over one sinner who repents. (StT James 4:8; 2 Corinthians 6:2; Luke 15:10)

The Greek word for joy, *chara*, means the awareness of God's grace, favor; joy. The Greek word for blessed, *makarios*, means supremely blest; happy. Could it be God gets excited when someone recognizes His Grace?

Jesus makes it even more clear that it is His Father Who is the Instigator of the celebratory 'search and **rescue**-d' mission. *"A certain man of you has one hundred sheep, and if he has lost one of them, will he not leave the nighty-nine in the wilderness and go after the lost one until he would find it? Then when he finds it he places it upon his shoulder rejoicing. And after he comes into his house he calls together his friends and neighbors saying to them, 'You must now **rejoice with me**...'" (Luke 15: 4-6, **emphasis mine**)*

As a shepherd carries a lamb... He will take up the
young to his chest... (StT Isaiah 40:11)

Matthew also records a confirmation it's our Father doing a happy dance over finding one lost sheep. The Hebrew word, *guwl*, means to spin around or dance under the influence of a violent emotion and is the word used for rejoice which corresponds to the Greek word, *agalliao*, describing Yeshua's exuberance. (StT Matthew 18:13; Luke 10:21)

Instead of being a stick in the mud, we should follow the rules of etiquette in Psalms 100 by serving the LORD with gladness and enter His gates expressing great happiness and triumphal singing!

Sounds like heaven has a continuous party going on.

Our Father still stands at His Door each day watching the horizon hoping this will be the time of a gracious welcome for each of us. When we approach Him with a contrite heart, He comes running to us. That's when the celebration for every person who returns to the place of their beginnings, our Father's House, can get under way.

If anyone hasn't already joined this shindig, the Father's always home waiting and watching to answer the knock of the humbled-hungry-returning-wander-off-ers with an enthusiastic *"Come on in! Let's eat!"*

Stirring the Golden Prayer Pot

Our Host Father, I know You will provide the necessary provisions, the hidden Mánna, for your handpicked ones to live this life in Your preferred-will.

Help me to feast on Your Secret Wisdom so I can taste the unique flavor of our covenantal ancestry in order to recognize when men are 'cooking The Book' to purposely mislead and deceive by dishonestly making changes to Your Written Records.

Thank You that Your Words are a fence of protection so we, Your covenant trusting people, will be kept in Your perfect peace; even in the midst of chaos. Without a revelation from Your word, folks don't have a moral incentive to stay on Your established path to green pastures with calm waters but go their own way. If they do nothing about the sin in their heart, they will have a lot of explaining to do when it's culling time for the living and the dead.

As I've gotten older, it's been hard not to think of myself as a dried up eunuch having nothing to offer. Help me to store Your treasures in others so the gift of future generations can be brought before **the King***!*

Second Serving: Chewin' the Cud

Open the gates to welcome the nation that is keeping the TRUTH. You will keep in Shalom Shalom the mind that has pledged covenant loyalty to You.

(StT Isaiah 26:2-3)

Jesus/Yeshua is The Light of the world: the one who follows Him will never walk in darkness, but will have the light of life.

(StT John 8:12)

"Go ask your grandma."

All I wanted to know was why Grandpa Herman opened the gate to let a particular cow go without milking her. To my seven year old mind there was only one reason why I had to trek to the house to ask Grandma, so I asked him, "Don't you know?" My quiet, reserved Grandpa sternly repeated, "GO. Ask. Your. Grandma."

Let me just say grandma's explanation made it *very* clear that even though in my eyes all cows looked the same they are NOT the same; some are bulls.

Thankfully a less graphic description of the distinction between the male and female than what my grandmother gave are the two Hebrew words used for the forming (*yatsar*) of man and the fashioning (*banah*) of woman.

My connotation of *yatsar* is our Father, as the potter, *squeezed* man's clay into the shape of his purpose. Since kings in the ancient Near East were considered images of the divine, it's fun to think God *hugged* Adam into service as His royal representative.

Knowing it was not good that Adam should rule alone, our Father *banah* an *ezer,* who would act as one yoked with him. *Banah* is used when referring to the making of palaces, a temple, and forms of art or for building a family.

In each of the twenty-one Old Testament verses where *ezer* is found it is in a military context of a rescuer and protector. Sixteen times it is for God as the shield and defense for His people against their enemies.

Blending these definitions, I imagine Eve as the Designer original fashioned to be a strong sanctuary as she walks with Adam in submission to their Father's Instructions.

On first sight of his fellow warrior, Adam exclaims the Hebrew for bone and flesh; *"Atsam* of my *atsam. Basar* of my *basar."* Owing to the fact *atsam,* means the self-same strength, Adam was affirming that woman was beautiful, yet no weakling. Besides meaning renewed vigor, *basar,* brings to mind of being the cheerful bearer of Good News.

Adam and Eve, male and female, were a reflection of our Father's nature equally mirroring His authority for continuing justice on the earth and were to expand His kingdom through their children. Written in ancient paleo Hebrew, *mother* is built into the word for *Truth* and becomes "mother of the covenant" with the addition of the Hebrew letter *tav* (a *sign* symbolizing to be yoked together or the covenant). As the first *mother,* Eve would be the giver of life to the covenant.

Way before Abraham, the first couple were to carefully instruct their household to keep themselves strong in relationship to our Father and to walk *The Covenant Walk* by doing what is good and right in the world and by showing mercy and justice to all others. By upholding their end of the covenant ensures that our Father's promises to them will be fulfilled and upheld forever as well. (StT Genesis 1:28; 18:19)

What could possibly go wrong with this set up?

A *rotten apple.*

The Garden's troublemaker used his corrupting influence to cause the Father's reflective image in Eve to turn sour.

The One New Man Bible's wording of this account in Genesis 3:1-8 makes it sound like we are eavesdropping at the tail end of a long running conversation between Eve and the double-dealing beast of the field: *"Really? Has God [Elohim] said, 'You will not eat of every tree of the garden.'"* Hoodwinked by the question, Eve doesn't refute it as one of those proud arguments, theories, and reasoning that sets itself up against the true knowledge of our Father. Instead of spitting out the poisonous brain food, she regurgitates the serpent's addressing of *God [Elohim]*, without the kinship of *LORD [Yahweh]*. The cunning creature, who had become discontented with executing his own created purpose, was about to succeed in having Eve do the same. (StT 2 Corinthians 10:5; Ezekiel 28:12-15)

After saying she and Adam could eat of the fruit of every tree except the fruit of the one in the midst of the garden, Eve added to what *God [Elohim]* said by saying they *were not even to touch it* or they would die.

Condescendingly the serpent replied Eve was not gonna die. *God [Elohim]* just didn't want her to reject His input. The troublemaker encouraged her to start making her own decisions of what is good or bad.

That did it. Miss Independent chose to no longer depend on God's authority, consumed the tree's eye opening hybrid fruit then gave some of it to her husband who was with her. After eating away their royal birthright, they were suddenly aware of their nakedness and stitched up some camouflage aprons just in time to hide from the *Voice of the LORD God [Yahweh Elohim]* walking in the garden. (StT Genesis 3:1-8)

Notice the original Hebrew words for addressing the LORD and God in brackets? Every other verse in Genesis 3, *LORD God [Yahweh Elohim]* is written except during the give-and-take between Eve and the serpent; *LORD [Yahweh]* is absent.

Like my innocent topside view of cows, *God [Elohim]*, and *LORD God [Yahweh Elohim]* may have looked the same but it is definitely NOT the same.

With all her walks with Him in the Garden, how could Eve ever start thinking *Lord God [Yahweh Elohim]* is stingy and withholding something good from her? Who was this character blurring Eve's perception of herself thus creating confusion in her genetics by modifying her generous *LORD God's [Yahweh Elohim]* True Name?

The serpent is usually called satan and his actions fit the description in Nahum 1:1 of another Hebrew word for satan, *Belial*, as the *wicked counselor* who imagines evil against the LORD.

When I looked up the original word for serpent used in this account, *nachash* has a meaning of shining one or glistening one. That seemed straightforward enough until I saw the root word for *nachash* [Strong's H5175] is also *nachash* [Strong's H5172] with the latter one meaning "to hiss or whisper."

I really needed that Hebrew to English cheat sheet.

From what Paul said about Satan masquerading as an angel of light, I'm going with my own inkling in saying Eve got distracted by a soft talking *shining object*. I can't help but wonder how long the exchange had been going on before Eve made the *Light Imitator's* downfall thought; *"I will make myself like the Most High"* her own? (StT Isaiah 14:14)

Was God's first daughter hungry when she was enticed to pick the forbidden fruit?

As the second Adam, Jesus came to undo the wrong the first Adam did. Possibly as it was with Eve in the first Garden it could've been the same when Jesus was led by the Spirit into the wilderness. We are let in on the fact that Jesus ate nothing while being *tested* by the Adversary for forty days and when *it* was finished, he was hungry. (StT 2 Corinthians 11:14; Luke 4:1-4)

The serpent could have been hissing his twisted truth every day for the entire 40 days but only his last hurrah was recorded. Playing on Jesus hunger, the tempter doesn't just tempt Him with food, but tries to create uncertainty in Jesus about His relationship with His Father by challenging, *"If you are the Son of God ..."*

A couple more times the glistening whisperer attempts to cast doubt on Jesus' lineage, but the True Son of God was having none of it.

Regrettably, God's first children took the bait. Instead of gaining godlike status by their own efforts, Adam and Eve stand stripped of the right to carry the strong tower Name of Yahweh where evil is inaccessible.

The One who is intimately acquainted with all the ways of Adam asks "Where are you?" The question doesn't make sense unless possibly the whereabouts inquiry was God asking Adam who had he been listening to that now his shame prevents him from coming into His presence? Perhaps God was asking why Adam had chosen to become the son of His enemy by believing Satan's half-truths and carrying out his new father's desire?

After all, doesn't God's question sound a lot like "Wherefore art thou" during Juliet's soliloquy lamenting why Romeo had to have the name of the family with whom her own was feuding? Makes sense to me because in the next line Juliet wants Romeo to deny his father and refuse his name. (StT John 8:44; Proverbs 18:10)

Knowing he was caught, Adam didn't take long before he threw out the first who's at fault. Of course Eve deflected to the serpent.

The blame game works both...er...three ways?

The Father of Truth doesn't let the father of lies off easy. The tempter was cursed more than all cattle and would have to crawl on its belly forever; consuming the dust out of which man was made.

To Adam and Eve our Father sort of said it was because of their broken trust in Him that they'll be returning to the basic ingredient from which they were made; *dust*. Oh how He wanted to spare them the *hard labor* the fruit of mixture germinates. But in their blind lust to become godlike by their own merit they couldn't see they were already a representation of Him.

Our Father continues by warning to be careful about walking by their *fleshy* desires, for now Satan and his ilk have the right to irritate and feed on their *dusty* nature. It is interesting that the Greek word for unclean, *akathartos*, (as in unclean spirits) means unclean in thought and life. To be clean, *kathairō*, our thoughts are to be free from wrong mixture.

Adam already had a job taking great care of Eden's weed free fenced pasture so *work* was not his curse. His sentence to doing the *hard labor* of a farmer's life meant now he would have to toil with thorns and weeds that will require sweating in the fields from dawn to dusk.

The light imitator slithers in the dark places of our mind's conversation to enhance his artificial illumination like a nightlight shines brightest where it's the darkest. This accuser of the believers uses our own voice to whisper twisted truth to darken our perceptions of another until we start doing his job of charging others with a fault thus injecting poison in our relationships.

After one service, I overheard two church character snipers *discreetly critiquing* someone who was standing across the sanctuary. Later, when Scott and I were eating lunch, I told him about the audacity of those two talking about another while we were all still in a place of refuge. Then it hit me what I was doing so I quickly added, "They should wait till after they get home to talk badly about someone like I do."

How's that for being the pot calling the kettle black?

Oh, I know it's wrong for a nitpicker to be looking for a speck in someone else's eye while having a plank completely blocking their own vision. It's not a coincidence the words behind speck and plank have the meaning that they are from the same material. Anyone trying to uncover the sin in others under the guise of helping is actually revealing they have the same sin but in a larger measure. There's no justification for them arrogantly passing judgment on another person when they are practicing the very same things they denounce. (StT Matthew 7:1-5; Romans 2:1)

The Judge Not Sacred Cow feeds off the fact most folks cut off the end of this story. Jesus actually tells us to remove the influence our plank has over our actions first *then* we are better able to help a brother remove his speck's power over him.

It's difficult to remove the per-*speck*-tive of sizing up another as a potential threat of sorts if we think our God given destiny can be taken from us to be given to them. David's oldest brother, Eliab, might have felt that way but being king was never his future in the first place. Oh he had the looks of a king so much so that both his dad and the prophet Samuel wrongfully thought he was God's sure fire pick. Even back then, external appearances seemed more important to people than what was important to God; a humble inner character.

Guess David's own dad couldn't imagine a royal destiny for his youngest boy because Jesse hadn't bothered to call David to the house. The Bible doesn't record Eliab's reaction to seeing his kid brother being anointed for the job he thought was rightly his, but a few verses later we can read Eliab's disdain for David when he arrives with the provisions Jesse sent for his older sons who were on the battle's frontline. Overhearing David ask what is in it for the guy who kills the uncircumcised Philistine trash talking Israel's army, Eliab begins to taunt his little brother. He insinuates David can't handle a big responsibility by asking who was watching David's *tiny* flock back home.

Was Eliab just shifting the focus off of his own evil heart by accusing David of having the same bad heart when he has the audacity to call his little brother arrogant who only wants to watch the battle for entertainment? What was his intent in trying to get David to believe a lowly flock watcher and serenader could never become a king no matter what the prophet Samuel had spoken? (StT 1 Samuel 16:6-17:29)

Sibling rivalry at it's finest!

Leah and Rachel are more Bible siblings who were first judged by their looks and where the oldest wasn't *chosen*. God looks upon the heart to judge a person's beauty sounds cliche' when we live in a fleshy world. After all it wasn't Rachel's great personality that caught Jacob's eye causing him to start flexing his muscles by rolling the heavy stone off the water well's mouth *by himself* then drawing water for her dad's animals.

It's been thought an ugly branch hit Leah because translations contrast her *tender* eyes with Rachel being beautiful and well favored. The Hebrew word, *rak,* characterizing Leah's eyes could be God's way of revealing the humbleness of Leah's inner character since it is the same word translated as the soft, tender answer used to divert an argument in Proverbs 15:1. (StT Genesis 29:10-17)

I question the ancient criteria for physical attractiveness since Hathor, the goddess of beauty, is usually depicted as a woman with the ears of a cow, with the whole head of a cow, or even as an entire cow.

Today, the golden calf of glamour god worship has made "Natural Beauties" rare and almost extinct. Toned thighs, tiny waists, and flawless skin on *photoshopped* women inundate us with ~~subtle~~ blatant standards of what encases the total woman with the emphasis on the *case*. Millions are spent on products and/or the extreme of plastic surgeries in an attempt to emulate the appearance of perfection because society dictates our worth is conditional on our "looking like a million."

Even though we know the truth of the lying camera, it's hard to switch off the critical comparison valve when we see one of those scrawny winged intimate apparel catwalk girls on TV while we're working at home changing diapers, folding laundry, or lots of other non-glamorous real world stuff.

We need to quit looking in the mirror or stepping on the scale to measure our worth. Scar equity, like sweat equity, is the physical proof we have increased value by the hardships we've endured as we strive towards the true lasting beauty that is pleasing to His sight. This character of spirit doesn't possess an exaggerated opinion of its own importance, but lovingly embraces its purpose for serving others.

Jesus emptied Himself of His own equality with God to take on the form of a humble servant whose human body didn't have the good looks that would make it the reason to be attracted to Him. He definitely bears the "scar-equity" for our spiritual restoration which is so much more than our original state. (StT Philippians 2:7; Isaiah 53:2; 1 Peter 2:21-25)

For the sake of an argument, what if Jewish tradition has it right that both Leah and Rachel were beautiful? So if it wasn't the looks comparison the sisters had to deal with, could it have been Rachel being her father and husband's favorite? It couldn't have helped Leah's marriage relationship that her dad, Laban, used her to dupe Jacob after he worked for seven years thinking only of Rachel.

Leah may not have been Jacob's first round pick, but she wasn't hated like we interpret the word. In Hebrew, the terms 'love' and 'hatred' are used in a comparative sense where hatred is not so much a hostile feeling but more of showing less love by withholding affection and covenant promises. So when the LORD saw that Leah was loved less in Jacob's eyes, He blessed her with children but Rachel remained barren.

Rather than being happy for her sister, Rachel turns her sister's baby blessing into a competition. She proclaims victory even though she cheated at first to get her own baby by giving her maid to Jacob. (StT Genesis 29:31; 30:8)

Interpersonal conflicts are nothing new to report however when it's between families or close friends the tension is escalated. The notion of Psalm 55:12-14 is David could handle a betrayal if it were an enemy boasting over and treating him like dirt. Only it was the very one he worshiped with and shared his life's intimate details who stabbed him in the back.

Paul had to deal with a fall out between *church* friends when he pleads with two women, Euodia and Syntyche, to quit quarreling and become friends again. (StT Philippians 4:2)

And just like that, they were.

I'm joking of course. We all know that you can win a war easier than win back the friendship of an offended person because their anger shuts you out like prison bars.

Who knows what the women were bumping heads about? Or if Paul at least offered a chocolate covenant of sorts to the women to help them put aside their bickering and agree the other one was not their rival.

A new generation of 'Euodias and Syntyches' don't handle their disputes privately nor alone. They libel the other to handpicked jurors for sympathy votes in their willful disregard of or disrespect for the authority of God's court of law. Lying by omission, not telling the whole truth and nothing but the truth, is breaking number nine on our Father's top ten *"How to Respect God and Play Well with Others"* list.

Of His ten covenant requirements, the ninth one is a prohibition of slandering the good name of someone you might just happen to be at odds. As any good father would, God does not want the reputation of any child of His to be handled carelessly by another. In a nutshell; we shouldn't be going around spreading gossip or try to acquire false testimony even by our silence in order to hurt the life of a fellow believer. (StT Leviticus 19:16)

It's not always easy to keep grazing on good news or bona fide concerns about someone instead of moseying into back-fence gossip. Maybe if we looked at gossip as an infectious disease we might be more apt to keep our conversations on the healthy side of the fence.

In Leviticus 14, the Hebrew word for leper, M'tsora is pronounced the same as two words, M'tso ra. The two words mean "finding evil" so from the earliest days the Jewish people knew the reference to gossip and slander.

The offering of the two birds (v. 4) represents the twittering and chirping of the gossiper and slanderer. One of the birds is killed, then not offered on the altar, but it is buried, as gossip and slander should be buried. The second bird is set free, representing the repentant sinner, forgiven by God, given another chance, then released to go and sin no more.

The root causes of this sin are jealousy and pride, because it breeds the contempt for others that lets them talk about others callously.

Joseph had a problem with this, based on Genesis 37:2, …Joseph brought to his father very evil reports about them

(His brothers). One word translated evil reports, with a second word meaning evil as modifying adjective. The repetition of evil makes that the superlative, very, in Hebrew. Bringing slanderous reports showed the wrong motive, when his goal apparently was to curry favor with Jacob, not to change the brothers' behavior. Joseph's sin of slander opened the door to the lies of Potiphar's wife." (The One New Man Bible)

A few wounded aren't concerned with what Solomon tweeted about not saying bad things about the king or rich people even alone in your bedroom; a little bird might tell it all to others. (StT Ecclesiastes 10:20) They use the Twitter Blue Bird themselves to publicize their falling-outs. Sort of contradicts the guidelines of Jesus in Matthew 18; if someone hurts you, work it out *privately* between the two of you.

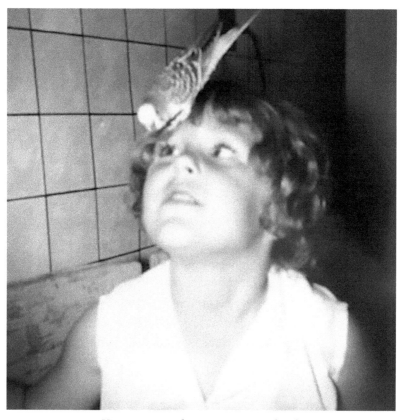

Happy, our parakeet, sitting on my head.

Instead of seeking to be our Father's agents of reconciliation, some follow memes that *excuse* the discarding of anyone simply because a derived benefit from them can no longer be received. Their *feelings* are more important than following the call to imitate Jesus by serving others without expecting to be served.

I'm not talking about abusive situations here. Not everyone has a healthy support system and there is no generic answer to fit every set of circumstances especially when children are involved. When I reached out for help where some abuse was escalating, I was told I deserved everything I got. Believing that lie, I continued to accept maltreatment from others for years.

In most cases, abusers never accept responsibility for *their* ill-behavior. Instead they sew together excuses to cover *their* sin or justify *their* bad behavior by accusing the other person.

King David pretty much broke every commandment yet he knew his transgression would be forgiven and his sin covered upon his returning to walk God's Way. He also knew he would not be forgiven if he continued to repeat the offense. Only a person who confesses AND stops doing what they did wrong will be let loose of their sin and given a second chance. (StT Psalm 32:1; Proverbs 28:13)

In the cases where the intimidator has seen the light of their sins, our Father may lead some like He did Ananias in Acts 9:14-16. Understandably Ananias balked at what he just heard the Lord say about going to heal Saul's blindness. Had the LORD forgotten this is the man who did **evil,** *kaka,* to His saints and had the authority from the high priest to bind all those who call on the Name of Yeshua/Jesus? Even so, the LORD told Ananias that he must be going because Saul was His chosen vessel to **carry** His Name before heathens, kings, and the children of Israel.

Saul/Paul's past evil actions against any who were of *The Way* still made him suspect in their minds. Barnabas took up for him by telling the apostles about Paul's enlightened conversation with the Lord on the road to Damascus and how he now speaks openly in the Name of Jesus. (StT Acts 9:26-27)

Kind of funny that Paul would later use the same Greek word for **evil**, *kaka,* when he warned Timothy about Alexander the Coppersmith. Alexander was vehemently opposing Paul and all the guys preaching the message of *The Way*. Paul was quoting Isaiah 59:18, Jeremiah 17:10, Psalm 28:4; 62:12, and Proverbs 24:12 when he said it was best to leave it up to the LORD to render to the culprit according to his deeds. (StT Romans 2:6;1 Corinthians 3:8; 2 Timothy 4:14-15)

No repentance; no restoration.

I'm thinking there was no repentance on Alexander's part even after Paul did the drill; if someone sins against you, confront him. *If he truly repents,* then forgive him. Even if he wrongs you seven times in a day, and each time he turns back to you saying, "I repent," you forgive him.

Paul also tells Timothy that when all had abandoned him, the LORD stood by and strengthened him so he could complete his purpose of telling the heathens God's message. Since the LORD rescued him from *the lion's mouth,* Paul was confident that He would rescue him from every evil, *poneros,* work and save him for His heavenly kingdom.

There's a difference between the two Greek words translated evil. *Kaka* is an inside job, the actions drawn from a morally-rotten character whereas *poneros* are the inevitable miseries and annoyances that seem to accompany evil.

Like Paul, we have all been (or still being) bullied by fiery-chatter-box lions (gossipers). But as followers of Jesus, we might need to ask a few questions before slamming the relationship door in non-life threatening environments. Such as what is the intent of our walking away or setting boundaries; to protect or to punish?

By design boundaries should have the intention of preserving relationships like a fire needs boundaries to be useful and to prevent it from raging out of control. But too often boundaries are selfishly misused by someone in their attempt to sooth their pain by controlling another. Their sudden banishment edict is a form of *silent* bullying and is not the way to God's justice that Daniel received in the pit where God shut the *lions' mouths.* (StT Daniel 6:22)

I'm still chewin' the cud on which situations it is okay that we walk away.

David once posted he was surrounded by *fierce lions* who greedily devour human prey with backbiting teeth that pierce like spears and arrows, and whose flaming tongues cut like swords. Was he speaking of the time he had to turn his back on his own brother when Eliab verbally attacked his God anointed kingly destination? After all, Jesus said in Matthew 10:36 that a man's enemies will be of his own household. Or when David had to flee from the king who was trying to kill him even though he regretted cutting off the tzitzits on Saul's prayer shawl?

In this century, Facebook has been used to burn many reputations when flare-ups between friends are publicized until "The Block" extinguishes the friendship. Nothing friendly about a disparaging fire of a biased account given to gain the advantage. Any story told first sounds true until the other person gets the opportunity to tell their side. (StT Psalms 57:4; 1 Samuel 17:30; 24:6; Proverbs 18:17, 19)

Mark 6:2-3 lets us in on how Bible small towns were like any in our present day where everybody knows everybody's background and business. Just because the town folk saw Jesus grow up with Joseph, Mary and His siblings didn't make them really know Who He was. When they heard Him teach in the synagogue on the seventh day Sabbath, they were offended by Him and closed themselves to His message.

The half-breed at the well, the social network of the time, knows how it is to be the talk of the town. This Samaritan woman may have gone to the water cooler at noon to avoid the looks and whispers from the goody two-shoes. (StT John 4:1-42)

One day a man surprises her by sending a friendship drink request. How could the *Jewish* Jesus see her, a *Samaritan*, when their ancestors had any possible interactions between them *blocked*? Still, even before He questions if the things spoken about her are true or not, He offers her the chance to be washed of her shame and no longer to be defined by her tainted reputation. His living water offer gives her hope that she will never have to come back to be ridiculed at the gossip pit again.

Uh oh. Jesus checks her *relationship* status; "It's complicated."

If we take into consideration that women were viewed as property in the ancient society in which she lived, our opinion of the woman at the well might need to be amended. Only men could initiate a divorce, so the fault does not lie with her if divorce is the reason for her five husbands. If she was guilty of the charge of prostitution, why didn't Jesus give her a repentance sermon then tell her to sin no more? This might not prove beyond a reasonable doubt that the Samaritan woman was not guilty of being promiscuous, but it doesn't feel right to interpret Jesus mentioning her husbands was to point out her sins since His Father **did not** send Him into the world in order **to condemn or pass sentence upon** it but that the world **would be saved through Him.** (StT John 3:17)

Possibly the LORD dislikes divorce because of the humiliation husbands put women through back in those days. That's why Joseph, not wanting to publicly disgrace Mary, had in mind of divorcing her quietly. (StT 1 Peter 3:7 Malachi 2:16; Matthew 1:19)

It only took one *"Insta-slam"* from a man who ignored the Biblical evidence to the contrary in order to frame Mary Magdalene as a prostitute after which a fast spreading smear campaign was on. From 591 AD, people have connected this Mary with the repentant sinner who wiped Jesus' feet with her tears. Restoring Mary's honorable reputation as one of Jesus' faithful financial supporters and being the first witness of His resurrection has been a long time coming.

I was, I AM, I always will be hasn't changed His view of how all His daughters should be treated. Just like Eve, they shouldn't be thought of as weaker than men, but honored as sacred vessels used in the temple or priceless vases one would protect from rough handling that could cause physical or spiritual brokenness. God won't hear the prayers of any husband who does not esteem his wife as his covenant partner.

There are seven things God hates with most of His animosity directed at pride. Eve might attest that it's because pride makes people want to rule independently from God. Plus, the proud have a tendency to exalt themselves by humiliating others.

Liars get a lot of dishonorable mentions. Maybe that's because God wants people to keep their word just like He keeps His.

The "No Killin' Folks" commandment uses the Hebrew *ratsach*, which is distinct from the Hebrew for kill, *harag*. Keeping it all in context of the time the rules were given, *harag* (kill) encompassed justifiable homicide, military at war and such. The use of *ratsach* (murder) was God's way of saying He doesn't want anyone deciding for themselves someone doesn't belong on this side of eternity then take the matter into their own hands of carrying out their own judgment call.

A heart that manufactures wicked thoughts and feet that are eager to carry out the evil plans pretty much reveals which family tree the person belongs to. Jesus bluntly called people who shut their ears to His teaching, *"children of the devil."* (StT John 8:44)

Issuing fake reports or speaking half-truths just to curry favor and win votes kind of goes with God hating anyone who likes to stir up trouble among fellow believers. (StT Exodus 23:1; Proverbs 6:16-19)

Medaniym, the Hebrew word for 'discord' used in Genesis 4:8 is like a battery operated quarrel that keeps going and going… Cain may have brooded on real or perceived injuries by Abel until he led his brother to the killing field. Joseph's brothers decided they would handle their 'family problem' in the same way but instead of killing him they cooked up another plan to make sure Joseph's dreams would never amount to anything. Even though they chose selling Joseph into slavery over murdering him, the brothers "killed" him all the same with the deceptive story they told their dad. (StT Genesis 37:18-33)

The names of characters and how the scenes have played out may differ, but I'm pretty sure none of us have escaped being adversely affected by those we love in one way or another. It could be the people we thought we couldn't live without seemed perfectly fine living without us.

The shining whisperer made the most of my parents' divorce and mom's lack of maintaining any connection with me as I grew older (and even now) to spread rejection's darkness over my spirit.

At five, four, and two years of age respectively, Paula, Kay, and I were too young to understand the reason we no longer saw our mom every day. Nor did we understand the court ordered guardianship that placed us with our paternal grandparents instead of staying with our dad.

Mom had moved eight hundred miles away so we only saw her a few weeks during the summer months. When she had three *new* kids it ingrained in my mind that we three girls were replaceable.

Even though he lived on the same farm, we didn't see daddy everyday which I took to mean I wasn't worth his time.

The close knit threesome we three sisters had was unraveled at a young age and we've never gotten it back.

Retrospection has caused quite a few sinking feelings as a flood of emotions overwhelmed me while writing this chapter.

None of us have achieved perfection in all of our ways so I in no way want to dishonor my parents or grandparents by zeroing in on their short-comings. I think family's would do well if they followed the example of Noah's two sons of walking backwards with the cloak of prayer to cover their families' faults instead of dishonoring them like the one son when he exposed Noah's *nakedness* to others. (StT Genesis 9:20-23)

Knowing I wasn't perfect, I didn't have to wait for others to point it out. I was already on the job with self-condemnation starting with thinking I was the cause of the divorce to fear of letting everyone down if I didn't do everything expected of me. So I kept busy and carried on as if nothing was wrong.

My warped perception that you had to work for the love you got was aided and abetted by Matthew 5:48 stating that we **must** be perfect. That word *perfect* is a kicker if you think like I did that it meant our Father has a 'no tolerance policy' for goofing up. Do you know how much pressure this conviction built up in me after I added pleasing God to my list of jobs?

Boy, was Jesus ever right in Luke 17:33 that whoever tries to preserve his life will lose it.

I was *losing* it.

There were occasions I resembled the forgotten potato filled pressure cooker left on the stove. I was six when I walked into the kitchen at the moment of the pot's 'having enough' detonation where potatoes went flying. That's what happens when the *doohickey* on the lid fails to do its created purpose of pressure relief. The pot, unable to release its internal built up pressure, exploded splattering its contents on the surrounding walls. Not being able to forgive, the rigid *character* of the pot pushed back with a vengeance.

My out of whack living may have been prevented if I had made use of my mind's *doohickey* in doing its job of refuting the pressures of distorted memories or even what actually happened. A fear of more hurts if I embodied a more lenient way of living built up. My *self-preservation* pot began to crack until my hot potato feelings spewed out on innocent loved ones which caused me to feel that I indeed needed to be replaced or discarded.

It's hard to look back and see that my pursuit of the all illusive state of perfection caused a lot of hurts, mine and others. Because it was *my* voice I was hearing, it never occurred to me it was the father of lies who was twisting words and perceptions in my mind.

If only I had known the Greek word translated perfect, *téleios*, has a meaning of spiritually growing up and fully developed in *sound judgment and discernment*. Maybe then I would've had the good sense not to leave my mind openly naked.

On the farm, the person at the gate was responsible for keeping the gate closed until time to let the cows in or out. In the Old Testament, gatekeepers were Levitical priests stationed at the House of God.

The fenced Garden of Eden was God's earthly house and as its first priestly gatekeeper, Adam, must have fallen asleep on his job rather than standing guard to shut the gate on the talkative intruder. Taking advantage of his access to True Father's Image Holders, the father of lies gave a misleading account about the mixed fruit tree's Instructions until Eve ignored God's protection label of "Do not ingest."

Satan hasn't diverged from the tactic he used on Eve to mess with how we perceive our Father's Teachings. At first glance, he makes the knowledge of good and evil fruit look the same as the Spirit's but it is not. The fruit of the Spirit germinates proper perspective of spiritual perfection and leaves the prerogative of determining what is good or evil up to God.

As gatekeeper over our thoughts, it's time we dress the part by putting on the full armor of our priestly garments starting with the turban of salvation that *girds up the loins of our mind* from the strategies of the devil. (StT 1 Peter 1:13)

The long tunics men wore with a "girdle" (belt) around the waist might be easy-breezy for hot weather and hanging around the house, but not when having to perform manual labor or going to war. In order to move quickly, the men would "gird up their loins" by tucking the hem of their garment into their girdle. We use a similar thought of "tightening our belts" when there's work to be done or a battle to be fought.

It's hard to be beautiful in the way we think when the enemy keeps our thoughts in a stew with a bombardment of verbal attacks. That's when we absolutely need to trust that God will not let us go it alone as if we are fatherless. By remaining humble before God we will receive power to resist the devil then can watch him skedaddle! (StT 2 Kings 6:16; Psalms 124:2-5; James 4:7)

Still, it is up to us to allow our Messiah's Light to wake us up from a mental stupor and use our God given authority to yank down every reckless reasonings that pits itself against the Life Giving True knowledge of God then shut the gate on arrogant farfetched hybrid lies of the devil that are full of bull.

Stirring the Golden Prayer Pot

Our Father, give me today the things necessary for my existence.

Even though my parents walked out and left me, You, Father, reached into my hiding place where I felt forgotten like a cracked pot, easily discarded and gladly replaced, to assure me I'm Your choice. You will not throw Your unique creation away!

Restore my inner being so I no longer relapse into my childhood rejection wounds made by the self-appointed 'somebodies' in our culture who have said no one cares about me.

Doing Your Family thing (Ekklesia), isn't always easy because there are times it stinks how people treat each other. You may choose to remember our sins no more when we accept Your reign over our life, but there are lots of folks who like to reminiscence and we become objects of their ridicule when we quit running with their herd.

Search me thoroughly to see if I'm in covenant with You. Scrutinize my anxious thoughts and let me know if they come from a hurtful way of thinking.

The Royal attitude does not look on nor speak garbage so let the words of my mouth be like a flowing brook of wisdom refreshing the hearts of others.

Don't let me depend on the external things the world calls beauty, but the the gentle quiet spirit of the heart for You beautify the humble and adorn them with a victorious crown when they assume their leadership position You've had for them from the foundation of the world! Awaken me to see heavenly realities that I have more warriors on My side than are on the enemy's. (StT 2 Kings 6:16)

Dressed in the armor of priestly garments, I will stand in my duty as gatekeeper to keep Your house a heresy and a hearsay free zone.

Thank You that whoever follows The Light that is Your Son will never walk in the darkness of personal effort, but will have the light of life to guide our thoughts with the covenant of peace.

Third Serving: Company's Comin'

And Y'shua said to them, "See that no one would lead you astray: for many will come in My name saying, 'I am the Messiah,' and they will deceive many."

(Matthew 24: 4-5)

Jesus/Yeshua is The Gate. If anyone enters through Him, they will be saved, and will come in and go out, and find pasture.

(StT John 10:9)

In one illustration, Jesus said the kingdom of heaven was akin to a farmer who sowed wheat seeds in his field. When his hired hands fell asleep on the job, the farmer's enemy crept into the field to plant darnel amongst the precious wheat seeds. As the crop grew, the hired hands noticed darnel among the wheat. How was that possible since the farmer had sown only good seeds in his field? This had to be the work of the farmer's enemy.

Not wanting to take the chance of losing any of the wheat if his hired hands tried to pull up the weeds, the farmer let both grow until harvest. Once the wheat had matured the farmer told the harvesters to collect the darnel first and tie them up to be burned. Only after that is done can the wheat be safely harvested and brought into the farmer's barn. (StT Matthew 13:24-30)

I would venture to say this same shifty darnel plantin' enemy visited upon our farm annually. In addition to having to deal with the weeds in our crops and garden, our grass pastures sometimes got overrun with *porcupine eggs.* That's what I called the small, hard, oval shaped cockle burr seeds that are covered with strong, hooked spines that I usually didn't see until they were stuck all over my clothing after walking or riding through the pasture. Removing the prickly invaders wasn't just annoying but painful since I always ended up with sore fingers when extracting the *porcupine eggs* entangled in my horse's mane and tail.

To keep Paul from becoming prideful on account of some pretty superior revelations, he had to deal with a few *porcupine eggs* of his own. To deduce if his thorn in the flesh was a physical ailment or not, it will help if we read his letters in a continuous fashion as we would any letter. Just before he mentions getting stuck with this *messenger of Satan,* Paul shares his concern that the Corinthians had snoozed instead of standing guard at the gates of their minds. By not staying alert the enemy was able to slip in to sow prickly weeds in their thoughts like he did with Eve. They were seduced away from their purity of heart in the Messiah then cheerfully accepted a man preaching a different Jesus from the one Paul had preached.

Neither Paul nor God had sent any of the charlatans to Corinth. Paul wasn't surprised that these phonies had transformed themselves into super apostles because their leader, Satan, disguises himself as an angel of light. All those heresy pushers, who were enjoying every opportunity to partake of meals and other advantages as they went house to house, would get their just *deserts* one day.

The Galatians hadn't done any better. Just like the Israelites were barely out of Egypt after God rescued them from slavery when they turned aside off the Way He had commanded, the Galatians chose an altered gospel over the sweet freedom Paul and the apostles had shared while the "hot donut sign" of their deliverance was still on.

Can't blame Paul for feeling agitated. After he planted a congregation in Truth, someone snuck into his field and gave a great performance of being a minister of righteousness.

Even though this minister was in it for his own greedy benefit, God chose not to remove the *thorn* from Paul's side. Maybe it was because God expected the congregation to grow up, quit relying on Paul for everything and get rid of the enemy's cling-ons themselves. Compare this to how God told the Israelites to drive out the inhabitants of the land He was giving them. If they did not, those same inhabitants would become annoying barbs in their eyes and irritating thorns in their sides by continually harassing them. (StT Exodus 32:8; 2 Corinthians 11:3-4, 15; 12:7, 17; Galatians 1:3-10; Numbers 33:55)

These are the reasons why I've concluded the *messenger from satan* was not some kind of sickness but a *menacing neighbor* who was pummeling Paul and why I think there are limitations on whom we are to offer hospitality.

Not everyone is to be welcomed into our house whether through the front door, tv, online, music or books if we want to hang onto the full reward we work towards. No covenantal greeting is to be given to anyone who exchanges the truth for the lie that says God approves of things His Word clearly records that He does not.

If the enemy/thief attempts a break-in, we are our own first responder. It is imperative to be on the ready by having Truth hid in our heart so as not to succumb to the captivity of false teachers who bring their unforgivable blasphemous works under the name of "Jesus" but fail the *test* of being a covenanted follower of the True Son of God.

Even though the Bible states we are not to trust every spirit but put the things done and said to the *test*, I couldn't find a simple multiple choice one. I used a few stories to come up with an answer key in deciding God is not behind the chaos that ensues when someone claims they are under the power of the Holy Spirit but can no longer manage their impulses. Jesus cast out demons from anyone who was not able to control their physical actions whereas the genuine Holy Spirit can be grieved, quenched or stopped. We are told not to extinguish the fire of the Holy Spirit or disregard prophecies but by all means use our judgement! Whatever passes the test of belonging to the original stock of His Spirit, hang on to that. Steer clear of evil in any form. (StT 1 John 4:1; 1 Thessalonians 5:19-22)

Those who protest they have been made free to act or think without hindrance or restraint of the law might need to rethink their position in light of Jesus' declaration to the *non*-Torah keepers on the Day of Judgment. They will have to depart from Him because He never *knew* them. (Used here, *knew* is a covenant term. Anyone not in covenant with Jesus will have to exit His presence.)

The sons of rebellion are like *porcupine eggs*; they cannot be culled by hand or they'll prick the fingers of the one who tries. A hoe is needed to throw them in the fire. (StT Matthew 7:23, 12:29, 31; Mark 3:27; Daniel 11:32; Luke 11:21-23; 1 Corinthians 16:13; 2 John 1:7-11; 2 Samuel 23:6)

Don't forget, anyone choosing to sneak over the wall by refusing to walk through the Gate must surely be a thief. Jesus paid for our citizenship so we could be *freely* born with full covenantal (constitutional) rights under His kingdom government. Anyone wanting to get in would have to wholeheartedly agree to the King's form of government and the laws by which it is administered. There are no rights allowing someone on the path to Kingdom citizenship to have one foot in God's country and the other in the world's way of doing things. (StT John 3:3; John 10:1)

Contrary to a lot of folks' perspective, God isn't the one making the choice of who gets into His forever Kingdom and who does not. Each person has the option of choosing or rejecting God's Way. Not wanting anyone to continue on their path towards eternal destruction, God is actually very patient and merciful in giving them chance after chance to repent. But if someone stubbornly makes their own choice of not being under His Teachings, they can't blame the God of justice if He is bound by His own *Law* to throw the covenant breakers into prison.

Both in the natural and the spiritual, laws protect the freedoms of law abiding citizens. Foreigners in the Bible were expected to obey the laws of the land they wished to dwell if they wanted to enjoy the full benefits of citizenship.

No shortcuts.

The Israelites were to work and pray to Yahweh for justice, provision for all, good health and good relationships in the city they were carried away captive. Their well-being was wrapped up in the well-being of the place they dwelled. (StT Jeremiah 29:7)

When ancient Israel was finally inhabiting their God promised land, they were to remember how it used to be with them in a foreign land and welcome any strangers who wished to become an Israelite. The strangers were expected to blend in as a law abiding Israelite and not try to set up a mini-country of their own within Israel's boundaries.

But what about us? What are we to do as individuals when we are doing our part but some "goats" butt in at the feed trough to take advantage of the law of hospitality? Especially when the utility bills go up and the grocery bill even higher without any household contribution from the freeloaders who are way past wearing out their welcome? (StT Proverbs 25:17)

According to Paul, stop feeding the moochers.

Ok, maybe Paul was firm but a bit nicer when he wrote that he, along with Silas and Timothy, had the right to expect hospitality yet it was more important for the three of them to lay the ground work for the way the Thessalonians should walk. (StT 2 Thessalonians 3:9-12)

Rumor had it that some folks were being idle and not earning their keep. Despite the fact they weren't supplying their own necessities they still expected to be fed. That's why Paul commanded that if anyone not willing to work shouldn't get to eat. He practiced what he preached by making prayer shawls. These shawls were worn as an outer garment that became a prayer closet (tent) by placing it over the head to shield the eyes while praying. I read this trade required Rabbinic training which I know Paul possessed but I'm guessing that so did Aquila and his wife, Priscilla (StT Acts 1.8:3.)

Sometimes it seems the folks willing to work get outnumbered by the ones willing to let them.

Thanks to his ancestors, Gideon had to deal with an invasion of Midianite squatters. The very name, *Midian,* means contention or strife and that's what God's people got when the prickly Midianites along with their cattle overran the Hebrew's farms leaving nothing but desolation.

It wasn't like the Hebrews weren't forewarned what would happen if they turned their backs on God's Instructions. They understood covenant better than we do; lots of blessings on the adherents of the covenant terms with the curses as a deterrent to breaking them. God's favor was on them if they walked in His statutes and kept His commandments to *do* them. But break the covenant on purpose by failing to do as He directed then they could expect terror, consumption, and to be consumed with inflammation. Whatever harvest they grew, raiders would eat. If after all that they still didn't listen to God, He would humble them by allowing all their hard work to result in crop failure.

After doing things their own way, the Hebrews once again cried out to God for help. He sends another no-name pop-up prophet with His message that seems to have accomplished nothing more than an "I told you so." (StT Leviticus 26:3-20; Judges 6:10)

According to Judges 2:1-3, one more time **I AM** (their True God) rescues a generation of Hebrews by bringing them into the land He had promised to their ancestors. He would *never break* His Covenant with them and their part of the bargain was to never make a covenant with the inhabitants of the land. In fact, they were to tear down the altars to the false gods but they didn't follow through. Instead, the children of Israel chose to party hard with the God-forbidden prevailing customs acquired from their neighbors. That is until their new friends started to torment them, then the Hebrews went crying to the very One they had rejected.

Wonder if the "children of Israel" label had anything to do with the fact they refused to listen to God in the same manner as a child ignores his parent's numerous warnings not to touch a hot stove by touching it anyway?

By touching yet another "hot stove" Israel goes crying to God with their burnt fingers. This time they don't get another "I told you so," but the LORD is about to kiss their boo-boo goodbye by sending His angel to awaken Gideon to his purpose.

Gideon's reaction to hearing that the LORD was with him and being called a mighty man of valor is priceless. It is as if he said, "Yeah, right. Sure He is. If the LORD is with me, then why are we having so much trouble at the hands of the Midianites? Where are some of those wonderful deeds our ancestors told us about?" (StT Judges 6:13)

*"The LORD **looked** at Gideon..."* God is always on high alert, constantly *looking* for people who follow Him with their whole heart so He can show Himself strong on their behalf. (StT 2 Chronicles 16:9)

Guess Gideon fit the bill because God said to him, *"Go in this your might and you will save Israel from the oppression at the hand of Midian. I AM is sending you."*

Gideon's name means "cutter down" so it makes sense that part of his purpose was to cull thirty-two thousand men down to a band of three hundred to help deliver the Midianites their eviction notice.

If Gideon used that newfangled math before going after his enemies, well, he and his men were going to die. But by using God's Covenant math of five going after a hundred enemies and a hundred men causing ten thousand to flee, Gideon could figure 300 X 10,000 = 3,000,000 antagonists vamoosing. (StT Leviticus 26:8)

Before taking care of the Midianites, Gideon was given his own "search and destroy mission." God was fed up with all the busyness of *the people's* religious meetings and pretentious worship with *their* altars to Baal so for the most part He tells Gideon to *cut 'er* down.

Following God's orders, Gideon uses his father's bull to pull down his father's altar and cut down the tree next to it that had been consecrated to this false god. On top of this stronghold, Gideon *correctly* built an altar to his True God then using the *pagan tree* for wood, he offered his father's bull as a burnt offering. (StT Amos 5:21-24; Judges 6:25-32)

What was the town folks' reaction for Gideon's *obedience to God* by cutting down the false religious relics handed down from their fathers? They wanted to kill him.

Folks take very seriously *their* sacred family traditions.

Did the ancient believers realize they were ignoring God's law by substituting *their own style* of worship? Maybe they knew *their festivities* came from false god worship, but they said a prayer that redeemed the bad stuff out of the celebrations? After all, didn't the "Feast of the LORD" declaration by God's real deal priest, Aaron, make the Golden Calf worship official?

> *"Moses saw that the people had lost all control because Aaron*
> *had let them get that way, and he realized their wild behavior*
> **had become a mockery in the sight of their enemies..."**
> *(Exodus 32:25)*

No amount of protesting, "But that's not what it means to me," is going to *un-taint* our witness if we put Jesus' Name on "harmless" God forbidden celebrations. The LORD's appointed seasons were never to be the Jewish way or the Christian way, but Yahweh's! (StT Leviticus 23:2)

Still, a lot of people think what is in their heart matters most regardless if their own beliefs are a contradiction of God's clearly defined decrees.

In matters of opinion, whose opinion counts?

The reaction to the *Gideons* trying to obey their God given command to cull the sacred cows from how God really wants to be worshiped hasn't changed over the years. The crowds violently reacted to the truth spoken by Joshua together with Caleb and wanted to kill them. Angry reactors to the truth succeeded in permanently silencing Stephen, ten of the disciples and Paul. Folks even got ticked with Truth Himself and wanted to throw Jesus off a cliff. (StT Numbers 14:6-10; Acts 5:40, 14:19; Luke 4:22-30)

Rumor has it the disciple John kept right on preaching from the pot of boiling oil in which he was plunged. Supposedly he survived without a burn and was banished to Patmos.

It is usually the Lord's own people who make fun of true prophets who try to teach knowledge and help those who have been weaned from milk to gain understanding.

Well, we better never outgrow needing *Him* like the children of ancient Israel. After the LORD *their* God had delivered them out of the hands of all their enemies, the children of Israel forgot about Him. As soon as Gideon was dead, they sprinted astray after Baalim and made Baal Berith their god. (StT Isaiah 28:9; Judges 8:33-35)

It wasn't any different after the first century gatekeepers were gone. As soon as Paul and all the original-covenant-keeping-disciples of Jesus died, the Sacred Cow breeders bolted out the gate taking as many quick converts as they could with them. Their prolific Heresy was made credible by mating Truth with error. Not to mention how some of the Original Writings were destroyed as a cover-up.

Jesus gave the call for everyone wearied and heavily burdened from these peace stealing religious rituals to come to Him. All we have to do is take up His yoke and learn from Him. His gentleness and humbleness of heart gives us rest due to the fact His yoke is easy and His burden is light. (StT Matthew 11:28-30)

Tractors may have been used on our farm but it still took long, hot, dusty hours to work the fields so being "yoked" and "finding rest" strikes me as an *OX*ymoron. Wouldn't ancient farmers have had it even harder since their *tractors* were yoked oxen in spite of the fact the team's synergistic partnership could pull ten times the workload than one could pull alone?

Recently, I learned that by harnessing a younger ox to an older one, the farmer could adjust the yoke *so the experienced ox carried the brunt of the work load.* This *yoke* discipleship training was not a painful cross for the greenhorn ox to bear, but a *grace* period while it learns to let go of its own way of doing things then humbly accepts its purpose in the farmer's plan.

If the young ox in training submits to the farmer's commands the load is light but if he stubbornly resists by *withdrawing the shoulder,* then the yoke is a heavy burden. A cattle prod is only used on stiff necked oxen that refuse to listen. If allowed to go its own way, believing the gracious farmer's instructions are optional or open to personal interpretations, the proud cow will convince itself that the farmer is okay with its rebellion. (StT Nehemiah 9:26-31; Acts 26:14; Ecclesiastes 8:11)

The childish tendency to use His Word for our own advantage could be why Jesus said to take time developing disciples by yoking mature followers with a spiritual newbie instead of making quick converts. The leader ox must not be a new follower of *The Way.* His spiritual immaturity might cause him to become conceited by his appointment to this high office then fall into the same condemnation incurred by the devil for his own arrogance and pride. (StT 1 Timothy 3:6)

Trained oxen will work for days without issue but will balk if the wooden yoke has a crack in it; they don't like the hair on their neck pulled. I don't blame them. I've been accused of being unwilling to submit to authority. There are occasions that might have been the case, but mostly those accusations came when I felt I was being led to plow an irregular scriptural row. I don't think I'm alone because I've heard of a lot of other folks stampeding away from the neck-hair-pinching-scripturally-flawed doctrines of various denominations. Jesus set us free from *doctrinal* legalism: so we must stand firm against receiving a yoke of bondage. (StT Galatians 5:1)

There were two objects nailed to the cross; the condemned person and a record of his crimes. Every decree of rules and regulations loaded on us were wiped away when the *record* against us was nailed to the cross *with* Jesus. His burden free commandments for Kingdom living were to continually be in force. (StT 1 John 5:3)

Despite this, it didn't silence the protestors' chants of "No More Torah!" *"The Pharisees were listening to all these things and since they were lovers of money they were sneering at Him."* Clearly Jesus didn't get the memo that it was no longer necessary to read or live by His Father's Rules because *"He said to them, you are justifying yourselves before man, but God knows your heart: because the one who is exalted among men is an abomination before God. The Torah (Teaching) and the Prophets were proclaimed until John:* **from then on the Kingdom of God is being preached and everyone enters it forcibly.** *And it is easier for heaven and Earth to pass away than for one* **vav** *of the Torah (Teaching) to fall. Everyone who divorces his wife and marries another is committing adultery and the man who marries her when she has been divorced from her husband is committing adultery." (Luke 16:14-18)*

The Greek word translated **forcibly**, *biazo,* is only used twice in the New Testament but both times positively. It means to use power to forcibly seize, laying hold of something with positive aggressiveness. When the revelation that the entire Hebrew Scrolls refer to Yeshua/Jesus is continually proclaimed, people will advance forcefully to get a share in the Kingdom of God by the utmost earnestness and effort!

To us westerners, Jesus seems to go off topic of heaven and earth would have to disappear before the second smallest letter in the Hebrew alphabet, *vav,* would be left out of His Written Truth to divorce and adultery.

His Hebrew listeners probably understood the similarity of what Jesus was teaching on adultery to the underlying message of Malachi 2:13-16. The people hearing Malachi's words were clueless of how the injustices they were experiencing had any connection with them being faithless to the *covenant wife of their youth* by running off with a *foreign woman.* Anyone divorcing themselves from the covenant wife of their youth (*Covenant Teachings*) by going a whoring after a foreign harlot (*Heresy*) was committing spiritual adultery.

The instant gratification of eating the Heresy Harlot's horse d'oovers still appeals to the fleshly desires of those wanting 'everything' now instead of storing up eternal treasures to be harvested in God's timing.

Whoa. If you think that's pretty strong language then read Galatians 5:12. Frustrated by corrupt teachers upsetting and confusing new believers by counseling that circumcision was necessary for salvation, Paul writes he wishes the agitators would *castrate* themselves. (Yes, that's what the original Greek word, *apokoptó,* means.) In 1 Timothy 4:1, he said some were departing from the true faith to follow the *doctrine of demons.*

Paul wasn't one to mince words. He wrote like a lead horseman who pushed the path's overgrowth out of the way only to let go after he rides on causing the branch to quickly recoil and smack the rider behind in the face.

Reminds me of the time my dad and Paula were riding lead and I was the recipient of more than one flying branch to the face. Accidentally or not, I question the motives and the smile on their faces.

Traveling down the road to understanding the True Way isn't always easy with all the conflicting denominational branches smacking us in the face. The Ephesians persevered in working hard and didn't tolerate evil overgrowth that tried to block or distort their faith with myths and tacked on rules laid down by men who rejected Torah.

By doing their own background checks, they didn't blindly accept men who billed themselves as apostles. They hated what Jesus hated; the works of the Nicolaitans which conquered the people through compromise with the world and tolerance of immorality. They may have gotten one thing right, but the Ephesians failed in the part of keeping their first love; the message of Truth. They had turned from the adoption of sons through covenant with Jesus after repentance of sins to accept wisdom that had come from a counterfeit spirit as if it had come from God. Even though these prophets prophesied falsely and the priests used their own self-appointed authority to subjugate them, God's people loved to have it that way. Jesus gave them the heads up to repent and do the works of their purpose they did at first; and if not, He would remove their menorah from its place. (StT Revelation 2:5-6; Jeremiah 5:31; Ephesians 1:4-14; James 3:15; 1 Corinthians 5:13; 2 Corinthians 6:17; Revelations 18:4)

Signs following doesn't mean someone has God's stamp of approval. There are a few opposers of Truth who can pull off the appearance of a miracle or two in the likes of the magicians, Janus and Jambros, who withstood Moses in Pharaoh's court. Some of these preachers of conformance to the world's image instead of the true Messiah's have caused the people to believe that their spirit was under grace so it doesn't matter what they do with their bodies. Instead of having their corrupt teaching culled before it became deeply rooted, these subverters grew in number until they had pretty much taken over. That's when the LORD had to tell the Real Truth *believers* to come out of this wrong set up so they don't share in the same sins and punishment when God's justice arrives.

The unrest in the world can elicit the self-preservation instinct resulting in people clamoring for an absolute sovereign who will be more than happy to use his authority to impose submission of the governed.

From His superior position in heaven, God finds it funny that these self-crowned elite kings of the earth collaborate for a worldwide revolt against Him and His chosen King. Yes, worldly power brokers resist His gentle yoke and what they wrongly perceive as its restrictions in order to advance their own evil tyrannical appetites, just like Nimrod. (StT Psalm 2:4)

Nimrod eagerly filled the divine role since people are easier to rule when they all *believe* in the same "god."

The Bible calling Nimrod "a mighty hunter before the LORD" can give the impression that God blessed his way of providing for the people. That misconception clears up knowing *Nimrod* means *"the rebel."* Aptly named when you understand that *mighty* used here means "one who makes himself greater in importance, behaves proudly, a tyrant and disrespectful." Insert that definition with *before* as "in the presence of" and Genesis 10:8-9 reads more like Nimrod was a tyrant who stood face to face with God and copped an attitude.

Under the guise of peaceful religious unity, Nimrod's counterfeit heaven's gate building program led a trusting people away from God's decrees. The "In Your face, God" tower of Babel was in direct defiance of God's command to fill the earth in Genesis 1:28, then renewed to Noah in Genesis 8:17.

God reacted to Nimrod's borderless society by separating the people through language which determined who all was going to reside within the boundaries of their new lands and territories. (StT Genesis 11:4; Acts 17: 26)

Borders between nations were God's doing consistent with His giving of the Torah as a boundary of protection. His Teachings are the arsenal we need to fight for **the** faith still today. Instead, we've let this spiritual weapon to be confiscated by the teaching it is *law* and no longer necessary.

David didn't want the WORD taken from his memory for his hope was in God's Ordinances. He promised to listen to, receive and obey God's Torah (Teaching) continually, forever and ever. Because he did his best to know God's Instructions, David knew he would live a life of freedom within its boundaries. (StT Psalms 119:43-45)

Fence shows God's wall of protection. Violence, devastation, and havoc will be unheard of within your borders. But you will call your walls Yeshuah and your gates Tehillah (praise).
(StT Isaiah 60:18)

Jude wanted to write about the first century believers common deliverance, but felt the necessity to write for them to earnestly contend for the rules and standards of kingdom citizens which were handed down through the prophets. He warned of Messiah deniers who had already snuck in. The fruits of their character are obvious; sweet grapes or delectable figs don't grow on thorny bushes or amongst prickly thistles. (StT Jude 3-4)

Daniel mentions a smooth talker, ticked with God's Covenant, who was flattering those who were willing to declare the covenant is wrong just to use them to build his army for attack on anyone who remains loyal to *the* faith of True God. Rather than conceding, the spiritually mature display the strength of their covenant and firmly oppose the deceiver.

Every freeborn again citizen of the Kingdom of God has been assigned with their own distinctive mission and must not sit back expecting someone else to take care of it for them. Their sharing of a song, a lesson, revelation… however the True Spirit leads is of vital importance to the ekklesia, the assembly of Kingdom citizens. Akin to how cows have one stomach but four parts with an equal work to do in a united purpose to give nutrients for the health of the whole cow, we all have our nourishing part for the life and faith of the one body of believers. (StT 1 Corinthians 14:26)

Yes, it's going to take the Kingdom's citizens working in tandem to prevent being blindsided by the anti-messiah spirit behind the unity of the One World Religion that's in the works as we speak.

Grandpa could consistently make good looking running rows so instead of training someone in the field to plant the peanuts he just did it himself. He at least tried to teach me the importance of getting the first crop row planted straight then all the other rows would be too. His secret was to not look back but fix his eyes on a reference point on the fence at the other end of the field. I may have passively *heard* him but I sure wasn't actively *listening*. If I had paid more attention maybe I wouldn't have run over my tractor's muffler when it fell off while I was looking back.

I'm surprised grandpa and daddy ever left me in a field alone.

How many other times had I not concerned myself with instructions about farm equipment beyond how to make the tractor go and of course the all-important stopping specifications? I think I was fourteen when daddy told me to take a bigger tractor than what I had been driving to a certain field. Since I was not familiar with it nor its attached equipment, I made him drive it on the busy highway and up the short incline to the field's gate while I followed in his pickup. As he was walking away, I told him the disc wouldn't fit between the gate. He argued it would. Turns out I was right. Daddy had failed to notice what I couldn't explain; the ends of the drag behind harrow were left in the down position making it extend out further on both sides than the disc. Not wanting to roll back down onto the highway, I revved up the tractor and put it in gear. Didn't think the field was the Kingdom of Heaven, but its gate was narrow and that busy wide road to it led to destruction; I tore up the fence. (StT Matthew 7:13)

In my defense, I'm a reading type of learner.

Glad God gave us Written Instructions (*Torah*, from the Hebrew verb *yarah*, which means to teach or point in a direction.) for walking a marker row for someone else.

According to Amos 3:3, two people can't walk together if they are not in agreement and translators differ on whether the Hebrew word used, *ya'ad,* means the two get together by *meeting* or by coming to an *agreement.*

Ya'ad, can mean betroth, which amazingly is another definition for *zugos* (translated *yoke*) that has the meaning of unity as in coupling marriage with the beam of balance.

Like just about everything else online, there are *strongly* differing opinions on the first century relationship between a rabbi and his disciples. For me, there were scriptures that seemed to support one opinion over the others.

Plainly I'm going with how a rabbi walked a marker row for his disciples. Every rabbi had a different *yoke* which was the authority of interpreting the Teachings. When a disciple (talmid) decided to put on a rabbi's "yoke of Torah" they were taking on the burden of keeping Torah to this particular rabbi's method.

"What is the greatest commandment in the Torah?" was the most important question a potential disciple needed to ask before giving everything up to get yoked up with a particular rabbi.

Similar to the farmer speaking as he walked along his yoked oxen, accepting the yoke of Rabbi Jesus brings us close enough to hear His gentle and humble heart so we can learn from Him and be like Him. This is how we find rest in our present lives. (StT Colossians 2:6; Matthew 11:29)

Although some rabbis could claim a godly lineage, they didn't allow Jesus' message to take hold of them. The intimate relationship covenant thing may be a clue as to why some don't have God's ear when they pray "In Jesus' Name." Praying 'in the Name' isn't so much saying the secret password as the sons of a certain high priest of Judea found out the hard way. They may have had a priestly lineage but the evil spirits they were trying to cast out of a man recognized the seven sons lacked the covenantal authority to use His Name as Jesus and Paul had. Instead of fleeing the man, the demons attack all seven to the point the men had to make a run for it. (StT Acts 19:11-16)

When a Pharisee questioned Rabbi Jesus' *yoke* with the question of which is the greatest Torah commandment, He answered *"You will love the Lord your God with your whole heart and with your whole being (Deuteronomy 6:5) and with your whole mind: this is the greatest and first commandment. And the second is like it, 'You will love your neighbor as yourself,' (Leviticus 19:18) the whole Torah (Teaching) and the Prophets are hanging on these two commandments." (Matthew 22:37-40)*

If folks are not doing the revere God with deference part then usually treating others with civility and respect in the ordinary dealings of life falls to the wayside.

Sour grapes might have a lot to do with dividing the body of Messiah up into different denominational groups. Some of these factions abuse God's grace by doing what they think is right without looking for guidance from His Word. The names of their gods and how they worshipped over the centuries may have changed but the blending of pagan worship with True God worship have not.

One encyclopedia states Christianity is probably the most syncretistic (the result of uniting different religions) of all the world religions. Although having Jewish roots, Christianity quickly came to absorb elements of other religions.

Like when Constantine, a sun worshiper, got the bright idea from seeing a flaming cross in a vision to put a cross on the shields of his pagan soldiers. There's a chance he fabricated it all to fire up his troops because later he decided to unite his kingdom by combining his sun religion with Christianity into one big universal church.

> *"At this meeting the question concerning the most holy day of Easter was discussed, and it was resolved by the united judgment of all present... it appeared an unworthy thing that in the celebration of this most holy feast we should follow the*

practice of the Jews,…For we have it in our power, if we abandon
their custom, to prolong the due observance of this ordinance
to future ages, by a truer order, which we have preserved from
the very day of the passion until the present time…Let us then
have nothing in common with the detestable Jewish crowd; for
we have received from our Savior a different way." *(Eusebius,*
Life of Constantine, Volume III Chapter XVIII, **emphasis mine**).

Constantine's disdain for the Family Tree in which Jesus and all converts belong, prove he did not follow the True Jesus but one of those "different" gospels Paul warned the Galatians.

Jesus never renounced His Jewish Heritage. As a Jewish Rabbi, He preached from Torah, attended synagogue on the seventh day Sabbath, and celebrated Yahweh's festivals (Especially Passover).

So instead of destroying paganism, Christianity adopted their deities, slapped Jesus' Name over them then celebrates as if God has given His approval on their cleaned up pagan holy days.

The opening story differs from my peanut hoeing one because the darnel look the same as wheat but there was no mistaking a peanut plant for a weed. The weeds in the peanut field needed to be cut down to ensure a productive life of the young peanut crop's underground *fruit*. On the other hand, attempts to remove the worthless darnel is risking uprooting both plants since its roots twist together with the wheat's.

During the growing season, appearances can be deceiving. Side by side, the darnel and wheat might look and act the same but are definitely not the same. Only at the harvest will the darnel be revealed as it remains pridefully stiff-necked while the matured wheat is humbly bowed from being heavy with life reproducing grain.

In the field of the world, darnel are fruitless swindlers so full of themselves they don't need God but will face His final judgement because they lack any grain of Truth. On the other hand, the good seed are the citizens of His Kingdom who produce life giving integrity grain that hasn't been corrupted by the influence of the unproductive deeds of darkness.

It is up to the gatekeepers to keep alert for any wrong kind of company comin' into the field in order to warn the people. It won't be his fault if anyone ignores the alarm and fails to do something for his own defense.

But if the gatekeeper keeps silent by not wanting to offend anyone and people in his field are taken captive by the enemy, then their blood will be on the hands of the gatekeeper. The gatekeeper must listen to what Yahweh has to say, then go and pass on His WORD so others can be saved and walk safely in freedom. (StT Ezekiel 33:3-7)

Stirring the Golden Prayer Pot

Our Father, I honor Your name by conducting myself as a commandment abiding free-born Kingdom citizen.

Well, that's my desire but sometimes I kick against Your prodding to walk Your Way by attempting to do things my own way. Still, I'm looking for the day I will no longer have to deal with the spiteful, thorny neighbors who mock when I fail miserably.

Plowing through the overgrowth loosens up a lot of harden dirt making it difficult sometimes to keep my footing. Prevent me from taking a slow slide into the ditch of legalism, Christian or Jewish, with the firm footing the gospel of Peace shoes give me. Yes, in the midst of chaos, inner shalom is mine and only comes from unbroken covenantal intimacy with You.

Since You don't yoke anyone up just to sit in a barn, I know there will be field tests in order to progressively learn Your Voice and to become a mature, growing thirsty learner of Your Truth. This requires lifestyle practice if I ever want to stand shoulder to shoulder to help carry another's burden to fulfill the requirements of the law of Your Son.

Expunge me of my wrongdoing, especially where I have followed the misleading teaching based on traditions fabricated by self-appointed inspired ones.

I know for certain that no one worshipping a false god has any inheritance in Your kingdom but happy are those who keep Your testimonies which is the root of our character.

As I learn from the things that happened to ancient Israel, show me how to stand as a gatekeeper and when to sound the alarm for others.

Fourth Serving: Settin' the Table

Then I said, Lo, I have come: It is written about Me in the volume of the book. I delight to do Your will, O My God. Yes, Your Torah (Teaching) is within my heart.

(Psalm 40:8-9)

Jesus/Yeshua is The Good Shepherd. The Good Shepherd lays down His life on behalf of His sheep.

(StT John 10:11)

My Grandpa Herman was a hard working farmer but also a man of few words or expressed emotions which was the reason his card to grandma one year was a bit of a surprise. The card's prose made grandma plum giddy as she shared with the rest of the family the written proof of her husband's affection for her. An embarrassed grandpa came to where I stood across the room and quietly confided, "I saw a card that said, *'To My Wife,'* so I bought it."

Grandpa's certainty that a greeting card company only sold cards with warm fuzzy feelings "to a wife" did not disappoint and I never revealed his secret that he had not opened to read the card's sentiment inside before purchasing... well at least not to grandma.

Many have bought our Father's *Card* without bothering to read His heart towards those He chose for His Son's Bride. They will not be given the covenant term *friends* reserved for those who treasure His *Card* then obey its Prose.

It is the glory of our Father to veil the true meaning of His Heart, but the honor of kings to lift the veil so to examine intimately His sentiments of covenant; loyalty, truth, and his merciful forgiveness of confessed sin. (StT Proverbs 25:2; Exodus 34:6-7.)

Jesus, mimicking His Father, gave the hidden meanings regarding the inner workings of the Kingdom to His *friends* but the crowd got parables. (StT Exodus 19:6; Revelation 1:6; Mark 4:11.)

In one of those parables, Jesus compared the kingdom of heaven to a king who had *cards* sent out telling everyone his best bull and the fattest cows had been slaughtered, and the table was set waiting for their arrival in order to start his son's wedding celebration. But the bunch of ingrates refused the king's request by giving one excuse after another. Many receive the invitation, but few are *eklektós,* the yielded believers who our Father certifies that the revelation He birthed within them will come to pass.

I've known from an early age that Jesus paid the price for our citizenship giving us the right to be reborn as natural citizens of His Kingdom. We don't earn this freeborn citizenship by adhering to His constitution but it is the way we show our gratitude by living it every day of our lives.

Still, it was surprising to me to find out Jesus wasn't just winging it until the time for Him to go to the cross. He never lost sight of where He was headed because He lived His Father's Word. "I AM Yahweh" established the end from the beginning and from ancient times the things that are not yet done. He declared His counsel will stand and He will do **all** His purpose. (StT Micah 5:2; Isaiah 46:10)

So everything concerning the True Messiah was written from the gitgo which includes the Law of Moses, the prophets, and the psalms. If anyone claimed to be the promised deliverer, their identity was to be verified by the Torah; the only trusted source for recognizing the real One.

Turns out that those who were very knowledgeable of the Hebrew Scriptures didn't fare too well when Jesus showed up. They misread the Word made flesh standing in front of them and refused to embrace Him as *"...The LORD Whom you seek will suddenly come to His Temple, **even the messenger of the covenant,** in whom you delight..." (Malachi 3:1, **emphasis mine**)*

In the same vein as the time God used Gideon to get rid of the burdensome yoke of their ancestor's oppressor, the Midianites, the religious leaders wanted *their* Messiah to free them from Roman rule by overthrowing the political good news that Caesar was the world's savior. (StT Isaiah 9:4)

I was a step ahead of these Jewish men seeing that I recognized Jesus as their Messiah as well as mine even though they could also read how Micah put His birth location on record: *"Bethlehem Ephrathah, you are small among the clans of Judah; One will come from you to be ruler over Israel for Me. His origin is from antiquity, from eternity." (5:2)*

From His birth in Bethlehem to His Exit outta here from the Mount of Olives summit, Jesus never deviated off His Messianic path. Where I missed it was in my speculatin' Jesus was *the message,* and not *the messenger of the covenant.*

As *the messenger,* did Jesus come to start a new Gentile religion or to *rev* up the original Covenant Kingdom of the Garden? Does the "gospel of Paul" supersede or differ from the basic message Jesus taught which was for people to turn around, accept His Father's rule and reign so all the kingdom citizen benefits would be theirs to enjoy?

It might be a jolt to some to find out the Gentiles were not Jesus' top priority but the missing *Hebrews.* He gave clear instructions in Matthew 10:5-6 to His *Hebrew* men not to go to any non-Jewish towns or even enter the Samaritan towns inhabited by people whose Jewish ancestors married Gentiles. They were to find and heal the *lost sheep of Israel* and tell **them** *"The kingdom of heaven is at hand."*

In Romans 11:1-2, Paul makes it clear that Israel has not and will not be replaced by a Gentile nation. He referenced himself along with the other first century believers as *"we Jews"* who were the first ones to have hope because of Jesus. Even though the Ephesians were Jewish, they were at one time in the world without Messiah which made them alienated from the citizenship of Israel and aliens of the promise of the covenant. (StT Ephesians 1:11-12; 2:12)

> *We are natural Jewish people and not sinners from the heathens:*
> *but, since we know that man is not justified because of works*
> *of tradition, but only through faith in Y'shua Messiah, we too*

have believed in Messiah Y'shua, so that we would be made
righteous by faith in Messiah and not by works of legalism,
because no one will be made righteous by works of legalism.
(Galatians 2:15-16)

"Jewish" is used here by Paul for the converts *from* Judaism that follow man made traditions tacked on to what is written in the Teachings. Greek intellectualism would have us interpret this verse that all we need to do is give a mental acceptance of Jesus and we are good for the long haul.

Repentance in Hebrew has the practical mindset of returning to God since sin is the going astray off the path of righteousness. God's mercy and bountiful pardon will be upon the wicked who abandon their own way and redirect their thoughts toward God's purpose for their lives. (StT Isaiah 55:7)

Anyhoo, Jesus must have shocked His men when later He announced that He had *other* sheep He wanted gathered into the original Hebrew Covenant people pen. He didn't say it was time for the Jews to enter into a "Christian" pen; it was the other way around. Or as Paul worded it in Romans 11:24, "heathens" were cut off from the wild olive tree and grafted **into** the *cultivated olive tree* (believing Israel).

The Gentile sheep were going to get in on the "Hebrews Only" covenant deal making all one flock following the Voice of One Shepherd. No longer would they be called "Gentile-God-fearers" not even "Gentile-Hebrews" but "Hebrews" with equal Kingdom Citizenship where no *hyphenated* names are allowed. This unity only happens for those who walk through the Covenant Gate we all know as Yeshua/Jesus. Can't get to His Father any other way no matter how many people of different religions think they can save their own lives by singing "We are the World."

The status quo of this forbidden to associate with group was about to change big time after Peter heard a Voice saying that he wasn't to declare unclean what God had cleansed. (StT John 10:16, 14:6; Acts 10:15-16)

Notice Peter was not given cleaning detail. We get into trouble when we interpret this verse as permission to make something God considers unclean by saying it has been "redeemed" or "it's under the blood." The blood of Jesus covers repented sin and should never be asked to cover a God forbidden practice.

Fresh off his triple rerun vision, Peter hears there are three Gentile men seeking to find him. The Spirit told him to get up, and not to raise any objections about going with them. (I hate to admit I'm still working on the "immediately she did what she was told without making a fuss.")

The Jewish Peter extended hospitality to the Gentile men. The next morning after arriving at Cornelius' house he states the obvious; it is contrary to law and justice for him, a Jew, to share hospitality with outsiders. But God had explained to Peter that he was not to call these men common or unclean. Still, Peter wants to know the reason Cornelius sent for him.

Cornelius explained that while he was praying four days ago to the very hour of afternoon they are now, a man dressed in shining clothing appeared with a message that God had heard his prayers and had seen his acts of lovingkindness so he was to immediately send for Peter.

Peter suddenly had a grasp on his vision. God does not show partiality, but in every shade of humankind the one who believes the message sent to the children of Israel (which all the prophets testify) takes the forgiveness of sins through Yeshua's Name. (StT Acts 10:34-43; Deuteronomy 10:17: 2 Chronicles 19:7; Mark 12:14)

In the midst of Peter's report on the things that happened throughout Judea and in Jerusalem, he says that Cornelius *already knew* the message about Jesus.

It's no surprise that Cornelius had knowledge of Jesus' crucifixion and *rumored* resurrection since it had probably been the top news story for quite some time. But with some figurin' of my own, I came up with the possibility he is the Gentile-centurion at the cross and should be included in the "we" in "*we* are witnesses" Peter referred to in Acts 10:39.

Before I go through how I got to that conclusion, I'm almost certain there very likely will be a few folks who might consider it a waste of time searching the rows of verses looking for answers to my many questions when I might not ever spot the sure nuff conclusive biblical one. Besides, there have been many martyrs who never thought to question some of the traditionally held beliefs as I have been doing. So does any of this matter if it doesn't change the faith we have in Jesus? I think it does in the aspect of protecting Truth for future generations so they can know and praise God for all He has done. Not to mention, sacred cows can persist if they are never called into question.

The Spirit of Knowledge

Redemption for all mankind was planned before Creation. The disciple John said the Word was in the beginning with God. Keep this in mind while reading John the Immerser as he spoke of a more important one coming who *lived long before* he was born. Of course John was talking about his younger cousin, Jesus.

God chose Abram to get the ball rolling on His Son's impending arrival. On Abram's part, he believed Yahweh's promise that his children would be as numerous as the stars and it was chalked up to him as righteousness. Believing in those days wasn't simply a mental assent but required a change in behavior; a *perfect* walk with God. Don't forget, *perfect* is walking with wholesome integrity in your all out commitment to put God's Way into action and doesn't mean you are entirely without sin.

When time came for the cutting of the covenant, the sacrificial animals were cut down the middle (except the bird) and each piece was lain opposite of each other.

Normally, the two parties making the covenant walked through the pieces in a figure eight, which is the infinity symbol. This bloody walk meant the covenant being made had no limits or end for either party; it was to last to infinity and beyond!

It wasn't unheard of for a substitute, a beloved son or servant, to make the infinity walk between the pieces. In any case, each person was in essence saying, "Just as this animal gave its life, so I will give my life if I do not fulfill my promise to you." Whichever side broke the covenant, their substitute would have to die just as the sacrificed animal had.

On the same day the LORD cut a covenant with Abram, *"a deep sleep fell upon Abram, ... And it was that when the sun went down and it was dark, there was a smoking furnace and a burning flame that passed between those pieces." (Genesis 15:17)*

The Hebrew for deliverance in Isaiah 62:1 is *Yeshuwah*. *"For Zion's sake I will not hold My peace and for Jerusalem's sake I will not rest, until its acts of lovingkindness go forth as brightness, and its deliverance as a burning lamp."*

Figured this gives credence to my thought that *Yeshua* is the flaming Word of Psalm 119:105.

Don't forget that Abraham was asleep so the smoking furnace and flaming torch emblem of the Divine Presence, made the infinity walk around the cut up sacrifice as the dual representative for both God and Abraham. This is why Jesus/*Yeshua* is *the messenger of the covenant* and would need to fulfill His priestly role at the exact same time as becoming like the cut sacrifice pieces and dying for us; the covenant breakers.

Because God seems to use certain places for historic events more than once, could Jesus have fulfilled His destiny on the very place Abraham took Isaac and the LORD provided a *substitute*? Jewish tradition has it all taking place on the Mount of Olives and it is said to this day, "The LORD Will Show Himself on the mountain."

No wonder the Mount of Olives was the main stage of Jesus' earthly walk. Its summit wasn't just a great place to view the temple, but this mountain's peak could definitely be seen from a distance and if I'm right that the Mount of Olives was considered "outside the camp" for the location of the *red heifer sin sacrifice,* then wow oh wow did the LORD see to it to show Himself and provide for us there. (StT Acts 1:9; Mark 13:1-3; Genesis 22:14; Numbers 19:1-10)

*"For while the blood of these animals is brought into the Holies by the High Priest to atone for sin, the bodies of these are burned **outside the camp.** For this reason then Y'shua, so that He would sanctify the people wrought His own blood, **suffered outside the gate.** So we should come out to Him **outside the camp where He bore His reproach.**" (Hebrews 13:11-13)*

There had to have been two altars since one is to be *"outside the camp"* and the other *"at the door of the Tent of Meeting before the LORD." (Leviticus 1:3, **emphasis mine**)*

Two locations would certainly clear up the discrepancy of King David's purchase price of fifty shekels of silver in 2 Samuel 24:24 and six hundred shekels of gold in 1 Chronicles 21:25. Not to mention the two different names of the land sellers.

If we all agree Jesus gave His life as a *sin* offering, then He could only have bore His reproach at the place ordained by His Father for the red heifer sacrifice *outside the camp*; the Mount of Olives. Any other location would nullify His sacrifice.

Centuries of traditions have placed the crucifixion and tomb at one place but where does the Bible place the two? I'm not sure.

Not being an expert in all the first century Temple happenings, I've tried to double and triple check to verify truth of the things I learned outside of the biblical narrative. Even though I have prayed for our Father's guidance to share His wonderful plan of redemption with nothing but the Truth, I am not infallible.

One fascinating Jewish folklore has the Mount of Olives as where God gathered the dust to form Adam and the place his skull is buried. That puts a different spin on the meaning that I always heard of *Golgotha* as the "Place of the Skull."

The Temple's threshold was built facing the Mount of Olives as was the tent's opening in the wilderness. This orientation for the altar afforded the large amount of water needed to clean the blood from the sacrifices to flow down into the Kidron Valley then to the Dead Sea.

The temple sacrifices are one reason I believe the Mount has to be the location of Jesus' Sin Offering Sacrifice. Like those, His 'blood and water' flowed down from His side to the Kidron Valley then into the Dead Sea.

Which makes me think the Dead Sea is the sea our repented sins are cast into. (StT Micah 7:19)

If we truly believe the only way to the Father is through His Son's sacrifice, then we should NOT be blaming anyone for Jesus' death. No one could kill Jesus without His consent; He laid down His life voluntarily. (StT John 10:18)

Every year, a few days before the time of Passover, the flocks of Passover lambs would arrive from Bethlehem to be paraded down the streets of Jerusalem. This is when the crowds would do a sort of rehearsal for the coming Messiah by throwing down palm branches and coats before the Passover lambs while singing *"Blessed be the One Who comes in the name of the Lord"* from the *Hallel (Psalms 113–118)*. It was during this Passover lamb parade that Jesus had His donkey ride in fulfillment of Zechariah 9:9. Matthew records that some of the crowd had no idea who the man riding a donkey among the lambs could be and were asking *"Who is this?" (21:10)*

Before Passover begins, the Israelites were instructed by Torah to clean out all leaven from their homes. This command of cleansing was rigorously followed leaving nothing unturned to find even the smallest crumb that might contain leaven. Jesus cleansed the leaven (doctrine) of the Pharisees by overturning tables and running out the moneychangers of His Father's house. Possibly Jesus was purging out the old leaven by dipping the last leaven containing morsel to give to Judas. (StT Exodus 12:19-20; John 13:26; 1 Corinthians 5:6-8)

During the four days leading up to Passover in which time the sacrificial lambs are inspected for blemishes, Jesus was being tried and pronounced innocent (without spot) by Pontius Pilate.

The crucifixion of Jesus on the Mount of Olives happening concurrently with the Passover sacrifices at the Temple, would give undeniable proof that Jesus was the prophesied Messiah and the broken covenant sacrifice.

I cannot find out who the priest was that actually oversaw the Passover lambs the day Jesus died on the cross. If it was the High Priest who stood watch during the long hours of the lambs being offered, then according to Leviticus 21:10, Caiaphas would have disqualified himself since a High Priest is never to rend his garment. Since there could only be one High Priest residing at a time, Caiaphas' act allowed Jesus to step into the role without breaking any of His Father's commandments. (StT Luke 23:14; Matthew 26:65; Mark 14:63)

At some point during the sacrifice of thousands of lambs, the High Priest would cry out, "I thirst." Then as the last lamb was offered, the High Priest would exclaim, "It is finished." Yeshua, our High Priest, would have called out at these same times. (StT John 19:28-30)

The scriptures about the sin sacrifice and how only a certain priest could handle the animal, finally make sense as to why the disciples didn't ask for Jesus' body. If anyone outside of the designated order of priests had touched Jesus then His sacrifice would have been made null and void. Joseph of Arimathea had to have been of the order of priests who could handle the sacrifice and Nicodemus would have been also of this order or at least considered the clean helper.

> "Then they took the body of Y'shua and they bound it in linen cloth with the spices, as is a custom of the Jewish people to prepare for burial. And there was **a garden in the place where He was crucified**, and a new tomb in the garden, a tomb in which no one had yet been placed." (John 19:40-41, **emphasis mine**)

Guess what? The Garden of Gethsemane is at the foot of the Mount of Olives. So it seems to have to be the garden in the place where Jesus was crucified if I'm right about the crucifixion tree being on the Mount of Olives.

Might need to mention there seems to be some significance about being buried with your ancestors. Jacob made Joseph swear not to bury him in Egypt but in his father's burying-place. Joseph left instructions for the Israelites to take his bones with them when God took them out of Egypt. (StT Genesis 47:30, 50:25) Could be Jesus needed to be buried where Adam had been?

Matthew's written testimony of the crucifixion has an important clue to the timeline of the resurrection. It became dark upon all the Earth from the sixth hour until the ninth hour, around noon to 3:00 PM. And about the ninth hour Yeshua cried out in a loud voice asking God why He had utterly forsaken Him. (27:45-46)

But wait! Before we rush to buy into Jesus was asking God "Where did you go?" there are too many verses that offer us the promise God will

NEVER quit on us. Jesus came to show us His Father and since He can't do anything but what He sees His Father doing, Jesus doubles the offer that under no circumstances will He leave us without His support either. (StT Hebrews 13:5)

At the time of His arrest, Jesus told Peter to sheath his sword because of His covenant with His Father Jesus could call *at once* and His Father would send more than twelve legions of angels to defend Him. If we figure 5500 men =1 legion then 12 X 5500 =… a lot of warring angels. But an angel rescue would not allow the story of God's kingdom to unfold in fulfillment of what was told by the prophets. (StT Matthew 26:53-54)

That's why I have a hard time accepting that Jesus *loudly* questioned His Father's presence in His hour of need. What exactly could He have possibly want everyone to hear since He said it so emphatically? Obviously those who stood there didn't understand what He was saying since some of them said he was calling for Elijah.

In our present day, some say Jesus was quoting Psalm 22:1 and a few others say David was just wrongly thinking God had abandoned him. Varied opinions on whether Jesus was speaking Hebrew or Arabic have come up with differing meanings. If Hebrew, then "forsake" wins the translation war. But if Arabic, then "was kept" is the winner. For all we know Jesus was confirming for all to hear that from the foundation of the world He **was kept** for this purpose.

> "And after Y'shua again cried out in a loud voice His spirit left Him. Then behold the veil of the Sanctuary was split in two from top to bottom and the earth quaked and stones were split, …And after the centurion, and those who were keeping watch over Y'shua with him **saw** the earthquake **and the things that happened,** they became very greatly fearful, saying, "Truly He was the Son of God." And many women, who followed Y'shua from Galilee to minister to Him, were there to see from afar…" (Matthew 27:50-55, **emphasis mine**)

Interestingly, I've found a few websites stating an earthquake fault line is found under the Mount of Olives, whereas there's not one under the other place popularly known as Golgotha.

Exactly what were *the other things* that the centurion and the crowds saw causing them to believe Jesus was the Son of God?

Not having the Jewish mindset or if we place the crucifixion in the wrong location we might miss the meaning behind the split curtain. Some contend the symbolism of the rent curtain is we now have direct communication with God and do not need a priest (Jewish or otherwise) as a go between. But Jesus had already taught His disciples how to pray in His Name straight to "Our Father." (StT Matthew 6:9-13)

Others think the rent curtain signified the abolishment of all things Hebraic, which would include the Hebrew Bible. But that meaning would negate the infinity and beyond meaning to God's Promises.

The curtain/veil is another thing that may have gotten lost in translation. Was it the Holy of Holies' veil that tore? Or the outer tall curtain? After going through a lot of different Greek and Hebrew words to decipher which curtain got ripped, I opt for the Sanctuary one. Especially since this outer curtain in Herod's Temple at the time of Jesus was 60 feet tall compared to 45 feet tall in Solomon's Temple.

Anyone else asking, "Why the 15 feet difference?"

When God is involved, nothing is happenstance.

If Jesus was impaled on the tree near the summit of the Mount of Olives, directly east of the Temple, seems to me that extra 15 feet of fabric would come in handy for the crowd to see a curtain, 80 feet by 24 feet, maybe a couple thousand feet away. Especially if the only light that shown during the total darkness hours was the menorah behind that tall curtain. Possibly the fiery altar helped light it up too. Still, even the smallest of lights can illuminate something near it when it's pitch black.

No one would miss feeling an earthquake taking place beneath them in order to possibly make the connection between Jesus and His Father. But what relevance would it have been to them if the other "things" they saw was God tearing the curtain at the exact moment Jesus died?

A common Hebrew custom, Kriah/keriah (meaning "to rip or rend"), requires mourners to tear an item of clothing at the moment of hearing of the death of their loved one. A cut is made on the left side of the clothing for parents–over the heart–and on the right side for all other relatives. The external tear is a symbol of the broken/torn heart within. Kriah/keriah, thus, also symbolizes the rending of the parent-child relationship, and confronts the mourner with the stabbing finality of this separation, expressed on his own clothes and on his own person for all to see. Not to mention the rending gives an opportunity to vent the pent-up anguish in a controlled, religiously sanctioned act.

Kriah/keriah is required to be performed while standing. The posture of accepting grief in Jewish life is always erect, symbolizing both strength in the face of crisis, and respect for the deceased. Job practiced this custom when he stood and tore his clothing the moment he heard the news of his children's death. (StT Job 1:2)

Through the stones being thrown at him, Stephen saw Jesus standing. Did Jesus rise from His seated position at the right hand of the Father to welcome Stephen home or was He practicing Kriah/keriah? (StT Acts 7:54)

When Isaiah saw the Lord sitting on a very high and exalted throne and His long robe filling the Temple, was he describing the Sanctuary Curtain as God's robe? (6:1) If so, would God tearing this curtain from the top at the exact moment of Jesus' death, be interpreted by all observers as this custom of the Father rending His clothes upon the death of His Son? Could the centurion possibly have seen the torn curtain when he declared that Jesus had to be the Son of God?

This explains how I deduced that Cornelius was the unnamed centurion and how he already knew something of Jesus but still needed Peter to tell him more.

A few first century details can get us pretty close to figuring out the rest of the story of when God raised Jesus. Jews numbered the days instead of giving them names except for the Sabbath. Some Jewish calendars number the months, and some have the names of the Babylonian gods which is similar to the Roman calendars with weekdays named after the Roman gods. Sunday is named after the sun-god, Monday after the moon-god, etc…

By using our present day Roman calendar to count from Good Friday to Sunday morning there is no truth in Matthew 12:40 that just as Jonah was three days and three nights in the whale's belly, so Jesus would be three days and three nights in the *heart of the earth.*

Anyone surprised that I have concluded the "heart of the earth" is the Mount of Olives?

After sifting through a lot of information, I found the Feast of Unleavened Bread lasted seven days, but Passover was a 24-hour period. All the signs I could find have Jesus dying on the afternoon of Passover on the 14th of Nisan of the Hebrew calendar. The last Passover lamb sacrifice would have been killed, at three o'clock, or, in case the eve of the Passover fell on the sixth day (Friday), at two. Jesus' death at three o'clock disproves the theory that He was crucified on a Friday before a regular Sabbath.

At sundown, the first day of the Feast of Unleavened bread began which was considered one of the annual High Sabbaths, but not the seventh day of the week Sabbath. The High Sabbath started at sunset on the fourth day of Passover week which explains why there were two *Sabbaths* during the crucifixion week.

To get to my resurrection time inference, I have drawn from when God told Abram his descendants would be enslaved and oppressed for four hundred years. (StT Genesis 15:13) What looks like a discrepancy and proof to some the inaccuracy of the Bible, is the verse in Exodus stating four hundred thirty years. I think God didn't count the honorable years the Hebrews lived under Joseph in Egypt *before* they were enslaved.

> *"And it was at the end of the four hundred thirty years, even the **selfsame day,** it was that all the hosts of the LORD went out from the land of Egypt." (Exodus 12:40, **emphasis mine**)*

No matter how you figure the math, the Hebrews *weren't in bondage* one day longer than God had said they would be. Jesus was in the tomb no longer than three days and nights. Neither was He entombed any less.

Keeping in mind the Biblical day is from sunset to sunset, then from His death at 3 pm on Wednesday, Jesus would have arose no later than 3 pm on the regular seventh day Sabbath. (Roman Calendar Saturday) Mary had to wait till Sabbath ended to go to the tomb on the "First Day of the Week" *which started at sundown.*

Jesus wouldn't have needed the stone to be rolled away to get out. Shut doors didn't stop Him from appearing in the midst of the disciples after His resurrection, which I assumed scared the daylight out of them since Jesus said, *"Peace be with you."* (StT John 20:26)

It was dark (Just after sundown?) when Mary arrived, saw that the stone had been rolled away from the tomb then takes off running until she saw Peter and John. After hearing her report that someone one had stolen Jesus' body, Peter and John raced to the tomb. John saw the linen cloths lying, nevertheless he did not enter. Peter enters the tomb *"and saw the cloths lying, and the face cloth, which had been on His head, not lying with the cloths but being folded up separately in one place."* Then John joins Peter in the tomb, *"he saw and believed…"* (John 20:1-8)

What was the big deal about the burial clothes that made him believe Jesus had risen from the dead? If Mary was correct and there had been an invasion of a body snatcher, couldn't they have removed the burial clothes and taken the time to refold them?

Lazarus' feet and hands were still bound with strips of cloth along with a separate head cloth for the dead, *soudarion,* when he was trying to obey the command of Jesus for him to come forth from his grave. Jesus had to say to whomever 'them' are to take off the grave clothes and let him go. (StT John 11:44)

If Lazarus and Jesus' burial clothes were strips of cloth then it was not a sheet of material that could be easily refolded. Most translations mention the face cloth being *folded* separately but I have my doubts it has anything to do with a supposedly ancient dining tradition of folding a napkin telling the servant he'll be back. The father is the Host of any meal served at his house and even though everything was eaten by hand in those days, I'm not convinced napkins (as we know them) were in use in ancient times.

The original word for folded in John 20:7 is *entulisso or entetyligmenon.* Both have a meaning to entwine or to roll around. The undisturbed windings of the facecloth could be the body of evidence that Jesus had risen right through its wrappings unlike the risen Lazarus who needed help getting out of his.

Filling in some of the details left out of Peter's report, it isn't hard to imagine why *"The Word of God was spreading and the number of disciples was multiplying greatly in Jerusalem, and **a great crowd of priests was submitting in the faith."** (Acts 6:7, **emphasis mine**)*

Was Caiaphas, the High priest who tore his clothes and accused Jesus of blasphemy, in this priestly crowd submitting to the faith after Jesus' Resurrection?

Again, many of my questions might need a few of those books that the world doesn't have room for. (StT John 21:25) When going outside the Bible for answers, I discard anything that contradicts Who the prophets say Jesus is. Their description that Jesus is the cornerstone is rock solid so I have no idea why the thought came to look up the meaning of *cornerstone.* Boy was I surprised to read "threshold" because the two didn't seem compatible since my front door is located in the middle of my house. Then I "accidentally" discovered front doors on some ancient houses were not centered, but located on the corner making the stone threshold part of the cornerstone.

The most famous verse about the threshold doesn't mention it by name.

> *"And you shall take a bunch of hyssop, dip it in the blood which is in the basin, and strike the lintel and the two doorposts...the LORD will pass over the door..." (Exodus 12:22-23)*

In the eastern world, the threshold was the most sacred part of the entire house. It was where covenants were made with one another and also with the household's gods.

The stone threshold also served as the home's altar where the father priest would have cut the sacrifice. We are used to seeing a basin as a bowl we hold in our hands. However in ancient times, the basin was built into the threshold of the door so the sacrificed animal's blood would flow across the stone and drain into the bowl carved into the stone for this purpose. It was this basin in which the father dipped the hyssop to cover the other three sides of the door's opening in the blood.

What if it was not a death angel crossing over the roof of the Hebrew' houses, but God crossing over the bloody threshold to enter into covenant with His people? Similar to the custom used for the marriage covenant where the husband carries the bride over the threshold or jumps the broom to symbolize his promise to take care of her, this could be what God was talking about when He carried Israel on eagle's wings and promised to supply "her" every need. (StT Exodus 19:4)

The stronger covenant partner provides the protection and supplies the needs of the weaker covenant partner. In all the forty years of wandering, not one of the 3 million people got sick or had swelling feet. Nor did their clothes and shoes wear out. Food and water were provided and their enemies destroyed. (StT Deuteronomy 8)

The Threshold Covenant is hospitality on steroids!

Rolling out the red carpet began from this custom of the blood of a slaughtered animal being shed upon the threshold at the arrival of a guest. Whether it was a bird, goat, lamb or calf to be sacrificed depended on the value the host placed on his guest. If the newcomer chooses to step over the sacrifice on the threshold then he is adopted into that family. To cross over a threshold and not hold to the highest laws of hospitality is to subject yourself to God's wrath. Stepping on the threshold rather than over it is more than extremely bad etiquette; it exhibits contempt for the host.

God showed how much He valued us by offering His only begotten Son so if we cross over the Threshold of His Son's shed blood, we are welcomed as part of His family. Jesus even told us He was the Door: if we accept His invitation to enter through Him we will be saved. Reconciled to be part of His family gives us the right to go out and find pasture but if we show contempt by disobeying the hospitality protocol and step on His Threshold, the wrath of God hangs on us continually. (StT John 3:36; 10:9)

A witness is needed for a covenant between two people so if one side doesn't carry out their required duties and wants to argue about their agreement then the witness can testify to the original terms.

Moses asked heaven and earth to be witnesses to God's offer of life or death, blessings or curses. Thankfully life is an open Book test. In case anyone was having a problem with choosing, Moses gives the answer with an explanation; choose life so both the people and their descendants may live on the fertile soil God promised to give their fathers Abraham, Isaac, and Jacob. (StT Deuteronomy 30:19-20)

Choosing life is to love the LORD by staying close enough to listen to His Voice then walk out what He said. Mostly we are taught that if we confess with our mouth Jesus/Yeshua and believe in our heart that God raised Him from the dead, we will be saved. But not so much that confession unto salvation is the Greek word, *homologeo*, meaning to assent by making covenant. (StT Romans 10:9-10)

The Greek word for confess in Romans 14:11 and Philippians 2:11 stating "every tongue shall confess" is *exomologeo*. This 'confession' is not accompanied by the making of a covenant. That's another one of those 'It looks the same, but it's not the same' Bible verses.

Every tongue might acknowledge God, but everyone won't have cut covenant with Him. Mere talk without a covenant commitment does not save anyone. Paul gave scriptural evidence to prove it is hazardous to our health to stay in ignorance to what it means to walk out our covenant. Anyone saying they have faith and act in a way that denies that faith won't get them anywhere except possibly sick, dying, or already dead if they take the covenant meal unworthily. (StT James 2:14; 1 Corinthians 11:27-30)

Yet great blessings belong to those who accept the invitation to the wedding supper of the Lamb! (StT Revelation 19:9)

Stirring the Golden Prayer Pot

You are our Father, our Redeemer. Your Name is from everlasting.

May others know that Your Son started out like You in every way, yet He chose to empty Himself of His own equality with You and the forever existence He had with You by taking the form of a humble servant, becoming obedient until death then triumphed over the grave.

I am determined to progressively become more intimately acquainted with Him, perceiving the wonders of His Person more strongly and more clearly, that I may know the power of His resurrection, share His sufferings as to be continually transformed in the hope of being lifted out from among the dead.

If I do nothing about the sin in my heart, You will not hear me when I call.

*A lot of true understanding has gotten blurred through heresies so help me to know how to keep **Your** Sabbaths and follow the terms of Your covenant just as You taught so I can be under Your protection and grace.*

Now protect and watch over all of us, Your Kingdom 'free born' citizens, who have set our love upon You!

Fifth Serving: Second Helpin's

You will have double because of your shame and instead of confusion they will rejoice in their portion. Therefore in their land they will possess the double portion: everlasting joy will be for them…All who see them will acknowledge them, that they are the seed which the LORD has blessed.

(Isaiah 61:7, 9)

Jesus/Yeshua is The True Vine and His Father is The Farmer. The one who dwells continuously in Him and He in them will bear much fruit, but unattached from Him, they can accomplish nothing.

(StT John 15:1-5)

On Saturday mornings in the early 1960's, western themed shows could be found on at least one of the only three television networks. I'd sing along with Roy Rogers and Dale Evans as they ended each of their episodes singing *Happy Trails*. "…Some trails are happy ones, others are blue. It's the way you ride the trail that counts, here's a happy one for you…"

Of course it's easy to have an upbeat demeanor when everything is going your way. Despite the fact Jesus told us we **get** to have tribulation, trials, distress and frustration, it still surprises me how life can be business as usual, and then wham, calamity strikes. (StT John 16:33)

Such was the case when Daddy and I were handling a simple move of cows from a pasture east of the highway to the pasture directly across it on the west side. Our large official "Cattle Crossing" warning signs were set up on both shoulders of the road and the moment traffic looked clear, we opened the gates. Everything was going to plan as the cows were following the first cow out of the fence protected field and onto the road. Our troubles began when out of the blue, a car topped the hill, sped up, and hit the lead cow that was almost completely across the road. Losing their leader in such a tragic way caused the rest of the herd to fearfully scatter.

We were too busy chasing cows to get the car's tag number as it sped off. If only the driver hadn't believed he could bypass the warning signs and our cows, then he wouldn't have sustained damage to his car when he killed our cow.

So much for the perceived easy life of a farmer. They know all too well that a sunny day perfect for plantin' can quickly fill with dark clouds ready to release a heavy downpour that makes the field too wet to work. Throw in some plant disease or pesky insects then a bumper crop year can change into a harvest that "could'a been better."

The book of Job is named after a man with a good weather life. It starts with a party going on. As was their custom on their own birthday, Job's sons took turns hosting their other siblings. There's no mention if the parents were requested to attend. Still Job sent for his children to come to his house for prayer after every celebration because he was *afraid* they had pridefully sinned against God in their hearts. (StT Job 1:5)

Job wasn't on the guest list of another kind of get together yet he was the topic of conversation. The children of God were presenting themselves before the LORD when our day and night accuser crashed the party. Instead of telling him to leave, God starts bragging about Job to Satan. Of course Satan challenges Job doesn't honor God for nothing. If Job, his family, and all he possesses were not shielded with God's personal security detail or if God ceased blessing everything Job's hand touched, then Satan alleges Job would sing a different tune.

God grants Satan permission to do what he wants with Job's possessions, but Job's body is off limits. With his permit in hand, Satan does his *job* on Job.

The first bad news courier hadn't finished talking about how all Job's cattle and donkeys have been stolen and the hired hands killed when another runner barged in with a sad tale of how lightening had struck the sheep and the shepherds too. Then he gets interrupted by the third messenger telling how the rest of Job's farm animals have been stolen when a fourth guy burst in with news of the roof caving in killing all Job's children.

Upon hearing the heart wrenching report of how a building collapsed on his children, Job stood up, tore his cloak (*Kriah/keriah*), wailed his famous lines about the Lord giving him what he had and the Lord taking it all away then fell to the ground and worshiped.

I disagree with Job assessing to God as being the culprit who had just stolen his goods, and killed his kids. Even so I have to give Job points for *immediately* praising the very ONE he thought had. I'm not sure how long it would take me to get around to "Praising God" if it had been the loss of my cows, donkeys, sheep, camels, employees, or the horrifying loss of all my children. I'm doubtful it would be the very minute I had gotten the news.

It's beyond me why people, who can read the rest of the story and know it was the accuser who received permission to pull all those bad things off, quote as truth, "The Lord gives, and the Lord takes." I don't find it comforting at all to think God gives you good stuff only to snatch it all away without notice or provocation.

How many kids overhear these words at funerals? We might need to rethink our consolin' words in light of how many of those same kids choose not to seek a relationship with a God who takes your family members and leaves you to fend for yourself.

Not sure if Job received a reprieve before round two when another day the sons of God present themselves before the Lord. God asks Satan where he's been. Satan answers that he's been roaming about the earth and observing its inhabitants.

Pretty sure God already knew the answer to satan's whereabouts so maybe the question was recorded to enlighten us to the fact Satan is NOT present in all places at the same time. Wonder if Peter was thinking of Adam or this verse in Job when he warns us to be on the look out because the devil is walking around like a hungry lion looking for someone to devour so we should not give him a way to go to work on us? Job's fear, the archenemy of faith, might have been the thing that attracted *where* the disaster would take place that day his world came crashing down.

For us, it might be hanging onto a grudge, feeding anger, cultivating bitterness, or giving resentment a place in our field that opens the gate to the devil to highlight our character flaws. (StT Job 2:2; Job 3:25; 1 Peter 5:8; Ephesians 4:27)

Job's integrity is unquestioned as he still reverently fears God despite the fact that Satan provoked God to take away His protection. Satan reasons that it's easy for a healthy person to love God, but afflicted with disease Job would curse God right to His face. The LORD told him how it was going to be. He was releasing Job into Satan's hand but killing him was off the table. With that, the Accuser left God's presence to infect Job's body with boils. While Job sat in ashes scraping the painful boils with a broken piece of pottery his wife found him...

Before anyone starts thinking, "Here it comes. Job's had about all he can stand, now his wife is going to use this as an opportunity to dump more rubbish on his head," let's check to see if we are overlooking something in her story. Until now, when Job has started *boil*-ing over, everything which her husband has run up against, she has suffered too.

Just because the Bible leaves her nameless does not mean Mrs. Job did not have any *sore* spots of her own. As any woman would, she had to be feeling she was walking through *death's darkest valley* David penned in Psalm 23:4. Her sorrow for the death of her child was real. Real times ten!

Having lost everything, her bereavement surely was compounded by money issues. Since the Bible said she *found* Job, I conclude she had been grieving alone which might've caused a strain on this couple's relationship.

Maybe her support group fled or gave annoying advice until she cried out to the LORD like Lazarus' sisters did about their brother. "If You'd had only been here, [my children] wouldn't have died." (Martha in John 11:21, Mary in John 11:32)

It's not hard to imagine if her thoughts and emotions were running rampant in her forlorn state. Mine have when lesser troubles sped in hitting out of nowhere. I felt God had passed me by just like His Son acted as if He was going to do with His storm tossed disciples. I even thought all the things were happening because God hated me. (StT Mark 6:48; Deuteronomy 1:27)

Of course I'm just speculatin' about Mrs. Job. She's been off-screen until she comes on the scene to discover the only thing she has left in life, her husband, is a walking *zit.* That's when she blurts out the words we assume means she is speaking from bitterness of heart, "Curse God and die." But was she?

The word Mrs. Job used for curse, is *barak,* interpreted as curse seven times (Four are in Job 1:5,11; 2:5,9) but used over three hundred times as a form of blessing. Proverbs 27:14 says it will be counted as a curse for anyone who *blesses* his neighbor first thing in the morning with a loud voice because the rise and shine *blessing* would either be annoying or for suspicious reasons. Possibly Mrs. Job's response came too early in the morning and Job took her wrong? Or could it be after all the two of them had been through, her heart cried out that at least one of them needed some relief?

Granted, Job said she was speaking like a foolish woman but did he know what he was talking about? Was Mrs. Job really encouraging her husband to give up?

Digging a little deeper into the Hebrew word for bless, *barak,* I uncovered its meaning is "to kneel." Picture someone blessing another by offering a gift on bended knee. Could Mrs. Job be telling her husband to humble himself before God's presence in adoration with the same risk factor as Queen Esther before she went outside the law's protocol in how to enter the king's presence; if he dies, he dies? (StT Esther 4:16)

The best conclusion in all my reckonings about Mrs. Job is we shouldn't be making any judgment calls unless we have all the facts and/ or have experienced the same things as someone else.

> *For we do not have a High Priest not able to be sympathetic with our weaknesses, but One Who has been tested against all things in quite the same way as we are but without sin. Therefore we should come to the throne of grace with boldness, so that we could take mercy and we would find grace in well-timed help. (Hebrews 4:15-16)*

There is some comfort in knowing the same heavenly messengers that were present to care for Jesus and minister to Him through His forty day wilderness test (StT Mark 1:10-13) are available to us in ours. But if I'm seeing the pattern correctly, God declares His delight in someone; (Job, Jesus...) then satan attacks, makes me sort of wanna tell God, "Please do NOT brag on me!"

Interestingly, Mrs. Job is not mentioned again. Job and some visiting church folks' futile attempt to figure out why bad things happen to good people fill several chapters while Job's wife ranks the distinction of a one-liner. Yet, if anyone knows the truth of Matthew 12:37, that your words carry the verdict of your guilt or innocence, it's her. In today's vernacular, this verse would read more like our Miranda Rights; "You have the right to remain silent. Anything you say can and will be used against you in a court of law."

My notion is that after all the negativity she got for one sentence, she decided it was best to keep her mouth shut. Is it possible she was quietly resting in Him while He renewed her strength?

To figure out how God possibly restored her, or any of His cracked copies, I decided to read in Jeremiah 18 about the potter's shop. That sort of helped. I had to do an online search on pottery making to get the gist of what Jeremiah saw.

Even though one of the potter's hands never leaves the forming clay on his wheel, the clay vessel can still become flawed and unusable. Similarly to how our Father is always there with His right hand embracing us during our formation, we can still become a flawed facsimile of His design for us. (StT Psalm 139:10)

The potter starts over the process of crushing, squeezing and molding the clay into the form in which he has need. After the pot has assumed its shape, the potter forces his hand into the inside of the pot, called the heart. If he doesn't work on the capacity of the heart, the vessel might look good on the outside but it can't be a source of supply thereby remaining useless. Only after He enlarges our hearts, will we be able to run the Way of His commandments. (StT Psalm 119:32)

The *mouth* of the pot will affect what is poured through it. If the *mouth* is broken, chipped, or cracked, then it can contaminate what is poured from the *heart*. The heart overflows in the words you speak; revealing what's within your heart. (StT Luke 6:45)

Once the pot has reached the potter's desired form, it's placed into a kiln to remove the water that has kept it soft and pliable during its creation. I can't explain the science behind what happens when the water is removed from the clay by high temperature, except the results are increased strength of the pot. The hotter the fire, the stronger the pot.

Pottery can become cracked and chipped just by being in use but some pots never achieve living out their destiny because they could not or would not go through the fire. They come out only *half-baked*.

Okay. My interaction with some 'cracked pots' led me to describe some of them as lacking common sense but I don't think it's a potter's term. It is true though that some pots are air baked or oven baked and by only going through the lower heat process they crack when stressed above their ability to hold together.

Mixing water with more clay to fill the pot's crack doesn't work because when put back into the fire, the patch material doesn't adhere. Bible time potters would fill the cracks with a mixture of powdered clay and blood that had been squeezed out of a *fasuka*. This was a tick like insect taken off of bulls or goats and kept in a small clay pot until their sticky bloody contents were needed. The pot is tempered, brought to the desired hardness or strength, by heating then cooling. However it is the adhesive power of the blood in the healing balm which makes the vessels strong. Just like the blood of Jesus binds up the wounds of the brokenhearted. (StT Psalms 147:3)

The potter repeats the process as often as necessary then puts his name on the healed vessel before releasing it for service. Pottery repaired in this way have been *reborn* and are called 'vessels of mercy.' The fact that clay pots thousands of years old have been found still intact, is an amazing testimony to that's pot's ability to take the heat. Vessels of His mercy are vessels of His strength.

Mrs. Job would have to have been resilient to give birth to children eleven through twenty. I wonder if God chose to fill her empty arms by single or multiple births. It is interesting that her original daughters had no names and had been only invited guests of their brothers but the *sequel* daughters received names and an inheritance. This broke the custom of sons alone receiving an inheritance which the bible only records it happening a couple more times with Zelophehad's five daughters and Caleb's daughter. (StT Numbers 27:4-8; Joshua 15:18-19)

If the meanings of the names of Jemima [light], Kezia [joyful aroma], and Kerenhappach [vessel of beauty] signify that after a calamity filled night, Job was joyfully and beautifully restored double for his troubles, then I have hope.

Yes, I believe our Father has declared restoration to all of Eve's daughters covenanted with Him with full and equal inheritance as His sons. Women denied this honor, or any honor, in the name of their religion might find it hard to believe what it means to be a daughter of covenant.

An actual descendant of Abraham, who was not able to stand fully erect for eighteen years, may never have heard the good news of her citizenship rights in the Kingdom either.

Jesus taught regularly in one of the synagogues on the Sabbath, but this day He sees her. When He calls out to her that she has been set free from her sickness and as He placed His hands on her, she **immediately straightened up** and was glorifying God.

Angered that Jesus healed on the Sabbath, the synagogue leader rebuked the crowd that they should come on one of the six work days to be healed and not on the Sabbath day. After *lovingly* calling the religious leaders "Hypocrites," Jesus did His question teaching thing by asking them if they didn't loose their cow or donkey from the stall and lead it out to let it drink on the Sabbath. His follow up question was about this **daughter of Abraham**, whom Satan bound eighteen long years. Was it not necessary to loose her from this bondage even on the Sabbath day?

His Words put all those opposed to Him to shame, but the whole crowd was rejoicing over all the splendid things Jesus was *doing*. (StT Luke 13:10-13; 14-16)

We don't know what kept Abraham's daughter from seeing anything more than dirt for eighteen years. Maybe the shining whisperer had been in her ear constantly reminding her of her dark past and it just kept adding up? Did the weight of shame she carried prevent her from looking up? Her constant bent over view of a fateful return to dust reminds me of the big picture window in the living room of an elderly nursing home; it faced directly across the street to the *funeral* home. Only her hopeless situation changed from death to life when she had a "Suddenly...God!" moment. (StT 2 Chronicles 29:36)

The *lifting of the head* is a Hebrew idiom meaning of one being restored to a place of honor. Our Father commanded a blessing in Numbers 6:26 where His approval of us is shown by lifting us above His head until His tranquil gaze captures ours and His joyful peace fills our hearts and lives. This is beautifully portrayed by a dad showing great pleasure in his child by whisking them up over his head until their eyes lock releasing the laughter that produces peace in his child's heart.

You must now see what manner of love the Father has given
to us so that we could be called children of God, and we are.
(1 John 3:1)

Ancient vineyard farming techniques capture the crux of Psalm 3:3 where only Jesus can lift a head bowed in shame. Even though we are more familiar with the translation of the Greek *airo*, as "prunes" or "take away," it can also mean to "lift up." If a grapevine is left to grow on the ground further out from the mother vine, it will make roots in the dirt at the point of contact. This will cause it to wither, especially in a drought. To protect the vine's future fruit bearing, the farmer lifts it out of the dirt and onto a rock.

Can't get much better in describing how the *Rock* represents the honor-restorer Messiah than what Jesus said Himself: Our Father is the True Farmer who cares for the young branches covenanted to the Deeper Root by propping up the branches on the *Rock*. He starts this early training by pruning the damaged or diseased parts with His Word. The pruning of any wayward shoots continues every year after so the healthy vine will mature as His disciple until one day glorify Him by yielding an abundant harvest.

A branch not dwelling in Him will not bear fruit and is not His disciple. It will be gathered up and thrown into the fire. (StT 1 Corinthians 10:4; John 15:1-8)

Anyone not allowing His Word to flow through them will experience a spiritual drought when sickness, unemployment, death of loved ones or whatever gets them thirsty for God to do something.

There were no signs of a dry spell going on when David's story began. He's out doing his regular field chores when a *"Suddenly, God…"* moment would change his life forever. (StT 1 Samuel 16:13)

Nothing in particular seemed to have changed on the outside after being anointed king by the Prophet Samuel considering David returned to his mundane shepherding job. Perhaps he became more in tuned to a royal way of thinking and what it meant to *"reign as king in life through the One, Y'shua Messiah." (Romans 5:17)*

By fully believing his covenantal right of protection, he killed the lion and the bear, oh my! Later, he was being his dad's errand boy when the business of going against Goliath came up.

Funny that this *child* and Israel's army had different reactions to hearing the taunts of Goliath. David recognized that this *uncircumcised* Philistine did not have the 'sign of the covenant' (circumcision) and therefore was not entitled to God's sacred promise of protection while the grown men were shaking in their boots (sandals?).

King Saul tried to discourage David by pointing out he lacked age and experience to fight the Philistine who had been a warrior since his childhood. But David knew the people who are in covenant with their

God will stand strong and get results. (StT 1 Samuel 17:17, 33-36; Jeremiah 1:7; Psalm 91:1; Daniel 11:32)

Goliath was going down.

Like many of us who had a dogged faith as children, life happened to David during the years before his prophesied king days arrived. Instead of his victory over Goliath putting him on easy street, David was thrown out on the street by the present king who went ballistic with a spear.

David may have journaled his ups and downs but he never wavered in his love for the Torah. In fact, almost every one of the one hundred and seventy six verses in Psalm 119 has a synonym for the Torah, such as *dabar* (word or promise) and *mishpatim* (rulings). Did he write verse 165 about those who love God's Torah (Teaching) have an abundance of peace and nothing along their paths can cause them to stumble while he was still being chased by people who wanted him permanently outa here?

God led David to the mighty, towering *Rock* of safety, the cave of Adullam.

The first helpin' we read of David's brothers was when they were in line in hopes one of them would receive the prophet Samuel's anointing on their head. Initially, not getting picked didn't sit too well with the oldest brother, Eliab but it's very likely all the stewing he did where his kid brother was concerned may have finally softened him up. In this second helping, Eliab joins the whole family to give David their full support. (StT 1 Samuel 22:1)

> "If it had not been the LORD Who was on our side when men rose up against us, then they would have swallowed us up alive when their wrath was kindled against us: then the **waters** would have overwhelmed us, the **stream** would have gone over our body: then the deliberately **wicked waters** would have gone over our body." *(Psalms 124:2-5, **emphasis mine**)*

On another one of those *life happening* days, we find David sitting among the ashes that used to be his home at *Ziklag*. This city's name pretty much clues us in on David's spirit possibly dwelling in a dejected place since it means being "pressed down" or "enveloped in grief."

Three days earlier, David was fired from his army job with King

Achish. While David and his men were on their way home, the Amalekites have not only burned the town down, they have stolen everything including the wives and children of David and his men. Now his men are speaking of stoning him. In spite of being between a rock (several rocks) and a hard place, David encouraged himself in the LORD his God. (StT 1 Samuel 30)

How did David go about giving spiritual CPR to himself when life knocked him down flat? Possibly David returned to his humble-harp-playing-sheep-watching-oiled-for-royalty-tenacious faith of his youth by offering *towdah*. One of seven Hebrew praise words, *towdah* believes Yahweh for the impossible allowing His power to work on our behalf as we praise Him with surrendered hands.

Despite his circumstances, David gave the sacrifice of thanksgiving and declared His works with rejoicing. By giving *towdah* praise, David was laying down his perspective of his many troubles. He then confessed his covenantal right to use Yahweh's name and believe that Yahweh will raise him up one more time. (StT Psalm 107:22; Psalm 71:20; Hebrews 13:15)

After asking the LORD what he should do, David got the Word to go after the Amalekites for he would surely recover everything that was taken from him. David returned to Ziklag so victorious that he sent part of the plunder to the elders of Judah, who were his friends. (StT 1 Samuel 30:8, 26)

Psalm 68:19 and Ephesians 4:8 confirm *Who* was behind David's victory: The God of armies ascended into the high places, turned *captivity captive* then gave gifts to mankind.

"Turning captivity captive" is a Hebrew idiom meaning "He turned the tables on your enemies in warfare." It's logical that *towdah* is seeing our victory before it happens because when I try to say *towdah*, it sounds more like the word of triumph, "Tada!"

One day while I was driving under the influence of the stresses of life, the LORD used a dead squirrel on the road to show me how to have an attitude of *towdah*. The only way I recognized it had been a squirrel was by its *fluffy-still-attached-to-its-flattened-body* tail. With each passing car's gust, its tail would arise as if tenaciously declaring, "Tada! I may be down, but I'm not totally out!"

This squirrel reminded me that no matter what happens, I should never ever stop giving *towdah* and to use my own mustard seed *faith **of** God*. I'm not talking from the perspective that a tiny belief the *size* of a mustard seed can make big things happen but the ability a mustard seed has to grow in almost any environment. Once a mustard seed takes root, even rocky terrain cannot stop its *true and living faith* because it has the ability to move *actual* stones out of its way.

The mustard seed has to do its own pushing to get the stone (mountain) out of the way as it rises towards the light of transformation into the tree (new life) the seed was covenanted with God to be. (StT Matthew 17:20)

With all the dark confusion in life and circumstances knocking us on our faces, it's not a time to be lacking in the faith department that's for sure. Now more than ever we need to let **the faith of God** shine in us. Since *our* mountain only responds to *our* voice, it's on us to use *towdah* praise to push our way up towards the light of a new life. People of all ranks will find their way home by the brightness of our rising.

It is conceivable that Jesus was talking about conquering kings leaving no stone unturned in their search for His concealed Truth when He said He will only give the secret manna to the one who conquers. (StT Proverbs 25:2; Revelation 2:17)

David may have had several helpin's of this royal food before becoming captain over an army made up of about four hundred men who had gathered behind him. At least David didn't have to worry that any of the men would be looking back with a yearning desire for the things left behind after they put their hands to the plow since they all had the misfit credentials of being in distress, debt and/or discontentment. (StT Psalm 61:2; Luke 9:62)

Adullam, which means 'a testimony to them,' would become the place for society's rejects to testify of what it meant to be in covenant by becoming victorious warriors who fought for their beloved king.

When two are in covenant, they first exchange robes and belts. By putting on the robe, they were giving their all to their "friend" and taking "within" themselves the essence of the other. The belt meant they would defend, protect and fight for the other. Being in covenant with God makes you a carrier of His Presence and no one can defeat you. (StT Romans 13:14; 2 Samuel 23:8-39; Romans 8:31)

The top three of David's mighty men either were in covenant with God themselves or David's covenant covered his *friends* also. (StT Job 22:30)

In one battle, Josheb-basshebeth slew eight hundred with his spear. In another, Eleazar fought so hard and long that his body became weak but he never let go of his sword!

The farmers fled when the Philistines gathered in a field of lentils, but Shammah stood and fought killing many Philistines. Yahweh gave His people a great victory.

Most of the fightin' David and his men did was for protecting the local farmers and not the 'time the kings battled' mentioned in 2 Samuel 11:1. On the latter occasion, it was not uncommon for a conquering king to kill any surviving relative of his defeated foe in order to prevent a future challenge to the throne.

Ignorant of the covenant between David and Jonathan, the person given protection duties of Jonathan's son hears that Saul and Jonathan are dead. In the process of fleeing, she drops Jonathan's son, Mephibosheth, which caused him to become lame. (2 Samuel 4:4)

Years later David gets to wondering if there is anyone left from Saul's family that he can show kindness according to his friendship covenant with Jonathan. Saul's servant, Ziba, knows that Mephibosheth was living in the house of Machir the son of Ammiel in Lo-debar.

With so many revelation gems hidden in the meaning of Hebrew names, I'm regretting skipping over the begats all those years.

The house, *bayith*, where Mephibosheth was staying can mean prison. Following all the connected Hebrew roots of Machir, it basically means 'he sold himself to death.' Ammiel's name comes from the root word, *amam* (to be held in darkness). Lo-debar means either 'no pasture' or 'no promise.'

Mephibosheth may have believed his name meaning, "breathing shame" or "despised," fit him by revealing contempt for himself with his "dead dog" reference when David arrived. Or he was playing the victim card. Sure he was crippled in both feet because of the actions of someone else, but in his dark place had he developed a "the world is against me" mindset?

If Mephibosheth was hoping for pity he was shooting too low. With one word from the king, he suddenly went from being put out to pasture with no promise of breaking out of his dark prison to eating bread at David's table as one of the king's sons for the rest of his life. (StT 2 Samuel 9:7-12)

Mephibosheth had every reason to shout, *"The LORD is My Miracle!"* (*Exodus 17:15*)

God had gotten rid of the accumulated burdens of his exile that made Mephibosheth's life miserable by bringing the lame one home again and turning his shame into honor all through the land. (StT Zephaniah 3:18-20)

Ummm…not so fast.

We first learn of Mephibosheth when the action of his nurse caused him to end up dwelling in a place with seemingly no future. The last we hear of him is when he's finagled out of his entire inheritance from yet another caretaker. The deception occurred when King David fled because of Absalom's plot to dethrone him by stealing the hearts of the people of Israel.

Ziba takes provisions to David and gave the reason why Mephibosheth didn't bring them was because he stayed in Jerusalem thinking now that David is gone, the people would give him back his grandfather's kingdom. For this newsflash David gives all that belonged to Mephibosheth to Ziba.

When David finally makes it home, the first thing out of his mouth was to ask a disheveled Mephibosheth why he didn't flee with him? That's when Ziba's deceit was uncovered. It was actually Mephibosheth's idea to saddle the donkey to ride with the king, but Ziba took it as his own and the opportunity to enrich himself by slandering Mephibosheth to the king.

David split the difference by giving each story teller half of the inheritance, but Mephibosheth told the king he was just grateful that David was safely back at the palace and to let Ziba take it all. (StT 2 Samuel 16: 3-4; 19:25-31)

Mephibosheth desired the king's *presence* more than his *presents*.

His answer to the king wasn't of self-pity. Sure his limitations had caused his need for assistance in going to David which resulted in a second helpin' of misfortune at the hands of another. He was no longer thinking 'poor me' but that the riches of his inheritance was being daily in the presence of his king.

Would I have answered the same? Am I willing to throw out

everything I could possibly obtain in this world as nothing but a pile of cow manure so that I may gain my KING? (StT Philippians 3:8)

Am I seeking His reign or mainly the necessities of life which is basically all about me? Am I coming from a sense of entitlement? Do I resort to complaining about what I would call intolerable *hardship* stones between me and my purpose? Do I expect others to pray them away instead of *praise pushing* them out of the way myself?

"God has not, and will not, abandon His covenant people" is not a one size fits all formula that keeps bad things from ever happening to good people.

I mean look at what all happened to David, who intensely pursued after what was on God's heart, and joined Him in walking out His will on earth as it is in heaven. Enoch's pursuit of walking the direction God was going caused him to one day sashay beside our Father all the way Home. (StT Isaiah 60:1-3;1 Samuel 13:14; Genesis 5:24)

If we don't refuse walking *with* God in *His* direction then this promise is ours; *"For in the time of trouble He will hide me in His pavilion. He will hide me in the secret place of His Tent.* **He will set me upon a rock. And** *now my head will* **be lifted up** *above my enemies all around me." (Psalms 27:5-6,* **emphasis mine***)*

Most of Job's book details the long discussion between his friends' religious critiquing and Job's own questions about a *just* God allowing his "time of trouble" before he sums it all up: *"I know that You can do everything (Matthew 19:26, Luke 1:34) and that no thought can be withheld from You. Who is the one who hides counsel without knowledge? Truly I have uttered what I do not understand, things too wonderful for me, which I did not know. ...I have heard of You by the listening of the ear, but now my eye sees You. Therefore I abhor myself, and repent in dust and ashes." (Job 42:1-6)*

Did you catch it? Job admits that he was talking about things over his head and takes back everything he said which surely included his "God gives and God takes" quote and calling his wife a foolish woman. But what was the sin Job was repenting since Job 1:22 said he had not sinned?

If sin only covers a visible action of breaking covenant with God Job is still in the clear. But Jesus said sin is in our wrong thinking. (StT Matthew 5:28)

> *"The heart is deceitful above all things, and desperately wicked;*
> *who can know it?" (Jeremiah 17:9)*

Job might not have charged God as having an unsavory character but his complaining spilled the beans on his prideful heart.

As *fur* back as I can remember, my mood was dependent on the circumstances. Sometimes I couldn't shake *the blues* when dealing with difficult periods and it wasn't like I had lost everything either.

After learning about the mustard seed, I realized it was up to me when I find myself on a rocky road to *choose* a joyful attitude while moving those stones out of my way. Of course I have the coworker of God's grace on my side to help produce a greater good out of hard times than I could accomplish alone being miserable. (StT 1 Thessalonians 5:18; Romans 8:28)

Like King David, Mrs. Job, and the squirrel, as a royal daughter of Abraham I choose to walk on a happy trail with my head up high even if my body and my mind may fail because God is the Rock and firm Strength of my heart and my forever Inheritance could not be better. (StT Psalm 73:26)

Stirring the Golden Prayer Pot

Our Father, it's hard not to resent the intruders called Trials along with their cohorts, Temptations. I'm still working on being happy that they've arrived for the purpose of digging into my heart to see if there is any hurtful way in me. But I would really like it if there was some short cut to character maturation that didn't involve sometimes painful tests similar to when a farmer separates wheat from the husks.

When You do permit the tempter to test me with calamities, lead me out of my brokenness into the season of Your favor where my time of mourning and depression will become my time of victory and gladness.

*Yes! Loose the bands on the neck of all Your captive daughters and set us upon **the** Rock to assume our position as leader as it was in our former Garden glory!*

Enlarge my heart as I listen to Your Word and make it my way of life. You direct Your specially chosen in everlasting covenantal truth.

For in the time of trouble You will hide me in the secret

place of Your Prayer Covering. You will set me upon a rock. And
now my head will be lifted up above my enemies all around me.
I will rejoice in my double portion and all who see me will
acknowledge that it is You that has blessed me when everything
comes about so suddenly!

Double Dippin'

You children of Zion, rejoice exuberantly! Rejoice in the LORD your God!
For He has given you the Teacher of acts of loving kindness and
1 the Teacher will cause the rain to come down for you,
the former rain and the latter rain as at the first. (Double Blessing)
[Surely goodness and loving kindness will pursue me all the days
of my life and I will dwell in the House of the LORD forever.]
2 And the floors will be full of wheat and the vats will
overflow with wine and oil. (Abundance)
[My cup is running over.]
3 And I shall restore to you the years that the locust, the canker worm,
the caterpillar, and the palmer worm have eaten, (Restoration)
[He will restore my soul.]
My great army which I sent among you.
4 And you will eat in plenty and be satisfied, (Never a Lack)
[The LORD is my Shepherd, I shall lack nothing.
He will cause me to lie down in green pastures:
He will lead me beside the still waters. He will guide
{This means more than just guide, it is also "in a path of blessing."}]
and praise the name of the LORD your God,
5 Who has dealt wondrously with you, (Miracles)
[You have anointed my head with oil.] and
6 My people will never be ashamed. (Respect)
[…righteousness for His name's sake.]
And you will know that
7 I AM in the midst of Israel, (Divine Presence)
[I will dwell in the House of the LORD. {Dwelling where He dwells.}]
and I AM the LORD your God, and no one else is, and My people will never be ashamed.
(Joel 2:23-27; [Psalm 23])

Dessert: Somethin' Sweet to Quit On

Now, Yahweh, do it again! Restore us to the former glory You had planned for us all along! Even though we walk the fields sowing our seed in tears and despair, You refresh our drought-stricken lives with Your rain so one day we shall come home again with a joyful shout of triumph carrying our abundant harvest!

(StT Psalm 126:4-6)

Jesus/Yeshua is The Resurrection and The Life: The one who believes in Him will live even if he dies.

(StT John 11:25)

Of all the famous talented singers born in Oklahoma, I was not one of them. Being neither famous nor talented, I can't explain how at the age of six and living on a farm I knew about *opera* or that the word meant work (both the activity involved and the purpose achieved). Did I even have an inkling that it was usually sung in whatever language in which it was composed?

My operatic dream came to a screeching halt the day daddy walked in as I was rehearsing at the top of my lungs my made up tune and language. He jokingly said something about me sounding hurt.

Where did my singing aspiration come from when no one else in my family can carry a tune either? In spite of that, I have not let my harmoniously challenged voice prevent me from bursting into song with lyrics applicable to any present life situation.

'Onward Christian Soldiers' was the song of choice during my daily chore of moving the milk cows off a certain grass field into the connecting larger main pasture. To be honest, I don't know if it was my droving skills that I could single handedly tackle the job at the age of nine or the cows were simply trying to *moo*-ve away from my barnyard *moo*-si-*cow*-l.

Now spontaneous praise happens on account of my heart boiling over with a song in the language of my King. How could I not when He is the composer of the music in my inward parts and He sings over me like a loving husband to calm all my fears and awaken me to new life?!!! (StT Psalms 45:1; 40:3; 103:1; Zephaniah 3:17)

Some wedding guests were singing Jesus' praises after drinking the fine new wine that had aged a few minutes past being plain water. Since this was His first miracle, Rabbi Jesus probably hadn't made a name for Himself that would've gotten Him on the guest list. It sure wasn't because a rabbi's presence was needed to conduct a marriage ceremony. Anyone could do that as long as there were two witnesses present.

Turns out a rabbi's religious duty at a wedding was to bring joy to the bride. Could Rabbi *Yeshua* have been the entertainment? The fact God poured more oil of joy on Him than on anyone else had to make Him the most animated Rabbi around. Jesus wanted us to be filled to overflowing with **His joy** as we continue living by His Code of Conduct. (StT Psalm 45:7; Hebrews 1:9; John 15:11)

Jesus had to have a lot of joy; you can't give something away that you don't have. Well, unless you're the government.

It might not have been His time to be responsible for Host duties when Mary told Jesus the wedding feast had run out of wine. Of course later He would host thousands of people by feeding the crowds on different occasions. Other times Jesus as host was more understated. Like when He asked folks, "How may I serve you?"

Well, that's how I interpret Jesus' question of "What do you want Me to do for you?" (StT John 2:4; Matthew 20:32)

Mostly I'm asking "What's in it for me?"

Peter asked the same question. Don't we all want to know what we get out of leaving everything to follow Jesus? Jesus reassured Peter that he wasn't going to lose out for making the realm of God and His judicial approval as the prime concern even over his family and home. By choosing well, Peter would recover many times more in this present life along with his transitory life one day getting absorbed into the life that is eternal sweetening the pot.

The *miraculous* health care plan Jesus offered those who had faith and the peace in which He sent them on their way wasn't too bad either.

Having the tax exemption status Jesus and Peter talked about in Matthew 17:25-27 would be great. Their conversation was about who had to pay the earthly kings' head tax; their sons or others? Peter said it was from the others. Jesus agreed the sons were indeed free but to go ahead and pay the tax so as not to offend anyone. Then He sends Peter off fishing.

It's all hunky-dory to read how Peter caught a fish with enough money in its mouth to pay both their taxes. But it's no laughing matter when it's my taxes, mortgage, rent, gas, insurance payments, groceries, utilities, etc, that's due and the fish aren't biting much less carrying money.

Or is it? What if laughter is the voice to our victory?

Nehemiah 8:10 records that the joy that God possesses and experiences will be our safe place; sheltered from trouble. Jeremiah chimes in with God's people will come home singing songs of triumph! They will be radiant with joy over the goodness of the LORD, over the abundant harvests of grain, wine, and oil plus healthy flocks and cattle. Their very beings will be like a watered garden and they will no longer languish. (StT Matthew 6:33, 19:27; Luke 18:29-30; Luke 8:48; Exodus 23:25; Jeremiah 31:12)

Grace and peace are multiplied in us through the true knowledge of the only God and of His Son. He handpicked us. Through His Divine power, He has implanted in us everything we could possibly need for life, to share in His Nature, and provided an escape from the depravity in the world. Our actions show our gratitude and cultivate moral goodness in our faith. Knowledge spices up our integrity, add in self-control which is boosted by patient endurance, then pair godliness with mercy towards our spiritual siblings. We won't trip up if these qualities are planted deep within, neither will we be fruitless or useless in the pursuit of the true knowledge of our Lord and Messiah. But if anyone lacks these qualities, they are blind to the mysteries of our faith and have a short memory of having their own past sins washed away.

The right hand of Yahweh does valiantly for those who put His commands into practice, you can hear the voice of singing and saving health in their private dwellings!

Just like a vacant house, our body deteriorates when there's no life in it.

One way to fill a "house" is by esteeming Jesus and keeping His Word. Jesus and His Father will honor the Torah Keeper by making a dwelling for themselves within him. If His Spirit resides in our bodies then "Temples R Us." (StT 2 Peter 1:2-11; Psalms 118:15; John 14:23; 1 Corinthians 6:19)

Kay, Paula, and I standing where the house we once lived with our parents had stood after it had just been moved to make way for Interstate 40.

*"For we know that if **our earthly house we live in of this tent** would be destroyed, we have a building from God, an **eternal***

house in the heavens not made by human hands. For indeed
we sigh in this **our dwelling**, longing to put on, for ourselves,
the one from heaven, then indeed, if we have been clothed we
will not be found naked. For indeed we, who are **in the tent**,
sigh, being oppressed, because of which we do not wish to be
unclothed but to be clothed, so that our mortal being would be
swallowed up by life." (2 Corinthians 5:1-4, **emphasis mine**)

The mistranslation of the Greek *mone*, and the Latin, *mansiones*, in
the verse where Jesus said there are many mansions in His Father's house
propagated the idea that we all would have a large physical building in
heaven that fits inside God's house. Of course the hymn, "Mansion over
the Hilltop" did nothing to arrest its widespread belief. These three words
win the "it looks the same, but it's not the same" prize except the latter
two have a meaning of staying, tarrying, abiding, dwelling and not of an
impressive house.

Why would anyone want or need to live eternally inside a huge
home? Who would they be trying to impress if everyone had one?

Jesus was speaking more of the particular portion of space in the
Kingdom of God where we rest or do our assignment. (StT John 14:2)

Precious in the sight of Yahweh is the death of His children who
withstood being absorbed by their lawless culture. Those who die in the
Lord from now on will be blessed with a short break from their labors
"for their works are following in company with them." (StT Psalm 116:15;
Revelation 14:13)

Unless you call camping at the lake to water ski a few days out of the
year a vacation, Grandpa didn't really take time off. But most Saturday
nights and Sundays he relaxed by playing cards at the kitchen table. The
type of cards varied and depended on which of my grandparent's friends
or family members were over at the house but table talkin' was always
on deck. Guess it was still one way the local news was shared as it had
been for years before people had television sets much less news channels.
Similar to the ancient hospitality custom where the traveling guest was
the host's source of news of what was going on in the *fur* country.

I have precious memories of sitting at the kitchen table while Grandpa
and Grandma talked about the "*fur* country" of their youth during a game

of double pinochle. As children, they worked alongside the **hard** hands on their own parents' farm.

It hit me a few years ago that it should be *hired* hands instead of how my grandparents referred to the help. Then again, *hired* hands are paid to do the *hard* work.

Can't blame my grandparent's dialect on the mixup of Rahab's line of work. Confusing her occupation of being an innkeeper with the oldest one of prostitution, is one of those "it looks the same, but it's not the same" situations.

The Hebrew word, *zonah* shares the same consonants with a "female who gives food and provisions" and a "prostitute." As for the Greek word, *porne,* describing Rahab as a prostitute in Hebrew 11:31, it has an alternate interpretation of an "idolatress."

Translators were rough on the reputations of some of our biblical heroines.

We first learn of Rahab when she offers hospitality to the two spies Joshua sent to Jericho. (StT Joshua 2)

Forty years earlier, twelve spies returned from scouting the Promised Land. All the spies agreed it was the best land ever. Then ten of them started sharing from their distorted perception of the giants. They saw themselves as grasshoppers next to them so of course these *small-thinking-mind-readers* **assumed** that they looked like grasshoppers in the eyes of the giants. (StT Numbers 13:33)

The other two spies, Joshua and Caleb, knew their God and what He is capable of carrying off and bound by covenant to do. They were ready to take action and attempted to rally the troops. The children of Israel don't need to be anxious. If the whole company will have faith in Yahweh and do what is right in His eyes, He will personally protect them on the way to new pasture and make it personally theirs.

The Israelites needed reminding that the stronger covenant partner provides the protection and supplies all the needs of the weaker covenant partner.

For emphasis, Joshua and Caleb repeated that they didn't need to be afraid of the covenant-less giants for no enemy could be successful against the children of Israel for God was on their side. But the rest of the Israelites were not convinced. Enraged, the majority moved to stone Joshua and Caleb. (StT Numbers 13:33; 14:6-10; Romans 8:31)

Fast forward and now new Hebrew messengers are able to hear Rahab paint a different picture of how her country men really perceived God's people. Instead of the big guys thinking about the little grasshopper humans they were going to stomp out, her people are living in terror because they know the LORD has given the Israelites their land and they have heard how the LORD made a dry path through the Red Sea when the Hebrews left Egypt. The men's hearts became even more fearful after hearing the news report of what happened to Sihon and Og, the two Amorite kings east of the Jordan River, whose people the Israelites completely destroyed. No one has the courage to fight after hearing such things, for Israel's God is the supreme God of the heavens above and the earth below. (StT Joshua 2:9-12)

Impoverished thinking got the Israelites forty years of walking a dusty trail.

I can't judge them too harshly. My own thinking still needs some daily *swiffer*-ing from tolerating inferior thoughts.

If I don't ignore "Do not ingest" warning labels, why would I keep chewing on anxious thoughts with the potential to poison my body? Instead of fretting, I need to make up my mind to be happy regardless of my circumstances, then I would have a continual feast that restores my soul. (StT Matthew 17:24-27; Proverbs 15:15, 17:22)

"Cleanliness is next to godliness" would be a great verse to keep my thinking under the 'all things' that should be done in order and not in a state of complete confusion and disorder. Except I've criss crossed the entire bible and never found this supposed verse. I did however find a blessing in Revelation 22:14 for those who are *washing* their robes. This isn't an already done once and finished laundry day experience. "Washing their robes" is an idiom for "*doing* His commandments."

For those caught in this 'act,' the One Who is the Alef and the Tav will reward them with His authority to enter His covenant gates and be granted to eat the fruit from the tree that gives provision for life.

Like Adam before his fall, we will have things to do in God's Garden, it just won't be arduous. Similar to Esther preparing for a year before she came before the king, there are things *the bride of Yeshua* (individually and collectively), has to *do* to prepare herself before her Bridegroom can return.

Our wholehearted commitment to show by the way we live, turning His commandments into deeds, is tested when it seems we are experiencing what Jeremiah saw; *a boiling pot* ready to spill out its evil [Torah-lessness] over the land. (StT Jeremiah 1:13-14)

This last days pot's ingredients listed in 2 Timothy 3 have been stewing for quite some time making it feel we are dwelling in the midst of Satan's field. Infected with selfishness, arrogant people will love themselves and the pleasures of the world more than God and mock those who have Torah in their hearts. These greedy boasters dishonor their parents, are hostile, slanderous, acting without restraint and haters of what is good and extremely ungrateful. God says this about those who feign a reverence for Him : *"This people honors Me with their lips, but their hearts are far distant away from Me: and they are worshipping Me in vain teaching (Doctrines) that are commandments of men." (Matthew 15:8-9; Isaiah 29:13)*

If the boiling pot example wasn't enough that things are going to get hot, Luke writes in Acts 14:22 how all His disciples will suffer a lot to enter into the Kingdom of God.

Weren't these Bible writers supposed to be Public Relations Specialists?

Surely there was a better good news plug than what Isaiah went with when he pointed out that people who refuse to do evil will be targeted in a time when truth is no longer being hoed (dug into). The enemy uses the non-kingdom citizens to unleash his weapon of word waves on anyone who starts living by Kingdom rules. Astonished by the New Lifer's change of values and their refusal to run with them in the flood of debauchery like before, the non-believers resort to criticism and ridicule. (StT Isaiah 15:59; 1 Peter 4:4)

> *The serpent spewed water like a river from its mouth* behind the woman, so that it could make her be swept away by a stream, **drowned in the waters.** Then the earth helped the woman and the earth opened its mouth and swallowed the river that **the dragon cast from its mouth.** And the dragon was angered on account of the woman and left to **make war with**

the rest of her seed, of those who keep the commandments of
God and have the Testimony of Y'shua. (Revelation 12:15-17,
emphasis mine)

David described his tormenters in Psalm 22:12 as strong bulls of Bashan [meaning shame], as they circled around him with their taunts.

The bulls and cows of *shame* sure get around. In Amos 4 we find them breaking down the fence around Torah which they thought would free them from being under its restraint. In their aimless luxuries, they had become fat cows on the fertile pastures of Bashan and had become **bull**-ies of the herd oppressing the innocent. These "cows" were told to repent, turn their minds around, and get back to walking in Covenant agreement so Yahweh could release the blessings that aren't mixed with troubles.

Daniel saw a horn warring against God's chosen ones and it was winning until the Ancient of Days made the judgment call in favor of His holy ones. The time had arrived for God's covenanted ones to receive royal power. (7:21-22)

Now that's what I'm talking about!

Doesn't having royal power mean we don't have to sit passively by when mob rule seems to reign supreme? Or do we just take what is dished out to us as most seem to interpret Jesus admonition that when we get slapped on the right cheek to offer up the other one to the slapper? Was Jesus a hypocrite? It doesn't sound like He practiced what He preached when Jesus did not turn the other cheek when He was slapped. (StT Matthew 5:39; John 18:22)

First off, the Bible is written in the language of Its Composer and the first listeners fully apprehended it from living in the honor and shame culture recorded in its pages. They knew striking someone's right cheek was to saddle them with shame.

According to ancient Jewish law, victims of abuse were to be compensated even if their pain and suffering wasn't physical but merely being insulted or humiliated. For a regular slap on the cheek, the victim would get one amount. But if the culprit used a backhanded motion, which slapping someone on the right cheek would require, his action was treated as being twice offensive so his victim would be awarded double.

Jesus could have been referring to a situation where the evil slapper was someone we have fellowship with and not so much to an oppressor of our rights or a foreign invader.

What was Jeremiah trying to tell us when he said, *"Let there be hope, that he give his cheek to the one who smites him, so he can be filled full with reproach"? (Lamentations 3:30)*

Which "he" in this verse is to be filled to the brim with shame? Is there to be hope for not strongly resisting an opponent because you will be rewarded double for your trouble? Or is the second "he" the slapper and it is his conscience that will be chock-full of shame for his mean and unworthy action?

Do we have the go ahead to cull the "Herd of the Perpetually Offended?"

Didn't Paul say to stay away from the ones who stir up contention, just as whipping milk produces butter, and twisting the nose causes bleeding? (StT Proverbs 30:33; 1 Corinthians 5:10-13; and 2 Timothy 3:5)

As much as I would enjoy slamming the gate on any anarchists' twisted noses who are creating a state of disorder due to the absence or nonrecognition of authority, we can't avoid contact with them altogether. Even though they continue with their divisive rhetoric or verdicts from their Court of Public Opinion, we are to live in peace with them. Well, as far as it is possible on our part.

Not everyone is responsive when we share the wonderful news of the free born citizenship Jesus paid for us all. Let God serve up His justice in His timing. In the meanwhile we have a 'seek and restore mission' to humbly serve up horse d'oovers from the King's Treasured Heirloom Collection whether the head shakers and the rolling-eyes folks accept it or not. Most real truth stragglers prefer the mooing of sacred cow fables and bleating myths that give approval to their Torah-less lifestyle. (StT Ezekiel 2:7; Proverbs 10:21)

God's equal-opportunity-covenant-blessings plan from when He created all humanity according to His likeness is still in effect. "All" means "all." No one was to be thought of as less deserving of His inheritance whether by their sex, color, or pecking order. We are to hold each other in highest esteem.

Honor works both ways.

Hard to know when it is time we can wash our hands of anyone who has hopped on the enemy's bandwagon of speaking against our God-given royal birthrights or if it is the time we make an effort at fence-mending.

Jesus broke down the spiritual antagonism fence between Jews and Gentiles so together we are built into a peaceful habitation of God. Clothed with Him there is no distinction of being Jewish or Greek, slave or free, male and female, but we are all one in Messiah Yeshua; true descendants of Abraham and heirs according to the promise. (StT Ephesians 2:14-15, 22; Galatians 3:26-29)

Not all siblings desire to create a peaceful habitation.

The farmer may have been happy when his young wayward son's heart was turned back to him, but his firstborn? Not so much.

When the older son was ready to call it a day's work he hears music and dancing going on back at the house. After asking what was going on, one of the hired hands answered that his brother was home, and the fattest calf has been butchered to celebrate his safe return.

The older brother angrily refused to join the party in honor of his kid brother so the father came out. During their conversation the compliant son pointed out how good he had been, never disobeying any orders by working hard those many years little brother wasn't around to help but off wasting the dad's inheritance. Yet not once did the father ever throw a party for him.

The father replied how he has loved the uninterrupted companionship with his firstborn but he was not living the reality that he was given his inheritance at the same time the younger son was given his. Yes, the inheritance led to the death of the kid brother, but now he's alive; lost and now found. So the father urged his firstborn to join the celebration and be happy. (StT Luke 15:11-32)

Instead of working for himself, the older son continued to live his life with a slave mentality instead of taking ownership of his inheritance.

It's a done deal. Our Father *has already* delighted to give us the kingdom.

It's not the hired hands, but the mature sons and daughters with the right to carry His Name who will receive the joyful inheritance of continually feasting at our Father's Family Table!

After every meal, Grandpa wanted "something sweet to quit on." I can't imagine anything sweeter than being called Yahweh's child, entering His rest, and sharing the inheritance with His Son. (StT Romans 8:17)

Then come the sour days I return to Prodigal Son mode. My focus is not on the Father, Jesus, or Heaven. No, it is more on the necessities of life which is basically all about me. Which of course fills my mind with anxiety because I've reduced life to the pursuit of my physical needs. That makes me no better than what the uncovenanted people of the world work for.

I'm probably not alone in this, so I'm writing this as a reminder for the *both* of us.

Our Good Host Father knows that we continually have need of things and supplies every single one of them, but we *need* to habitually seek His kingdom first. In our exiled state, our path should be charted by faith, not by what our eyes can see. I will hold on to faith in God and choose not to be distressed because all my **needs** are provided *according to His riches* not mine.

He can handle it, all the silver and all the gold in this world already belong to Him not to mention He has cattle grazing over a thousand hills. (StT Luke 12:29-32; Philippians 4:19; Haggai 2:8; Psalm 50:10)

I don't think God's economy ever goes through a recession where He has to sell a cow on our behalf, but I do remember going to the stock yard early one morning with grandpa to sell some cows. We returned home in time to catch the farm report at noon. Both of us were surprised to see ourselves on television. We had not seen the news camera filming us while watching the auction.

Selling cows was part of the job of being a farmer. Kings in the Bible had an odd requirement; they had a set time of the year to go off to battle.

Might this battling kings thing have something to do as to why God had left a few nations to test and to teach the generations of Israelites who didn't know anything about war? (StT 1 Chronicles 20:1; Judges 3:1-2)

Unlike their ancestors who only thought from their bondage perspective instead of trusting His Words of Promise, could it be God wanted them to learn how *to be* and *think* like kings?

The All-Knowing One set up His rules for a king years before the people would reject His rule over them. The king must trust in the Most High and through *checed* (covenant loyalty) with Him, he will not deviate from the right course. (StT Psalm 21:7)

First, God would be the Chooser and the *chosen* man for the position would be a citizen of His Covenant Community and not a foreigner.

The king wasn't to look to Egypt for building his army but trust in the LORD's protection. Multiple wives or hoarding riches that would turn his heart away from God's was also a big no-no.

The king must write out a copy of Torah for himself while the Levitical priests look on to make sure he gets it right. He was to keep it with him and read it every day so that he will learn to revere the LORD, keep all the words of Torah, and remember all His decrees in order to *do* them. That way he won't get all high and mighty and start mistreating and oppressing his kingdom brothers. (StT 1 Samuel 8:7; Psalm 106:24; Deuteronomy 17:14-20)

Those qualifications sound a lot like the ones for the office of elder who must have an honorable reputation outside the congregation, only one wife, sensible, *hospitable*, able to teach Torah, not a bully, quick tempered, or greedy. Neither a spiritual newbie that he might *get too big for his britches,* which was my grandparent's way of saying someone was acting more important than they really are. (StT 1 Timothy 3:1-7)

We should have the mind of Messiah that only does His will and walks His walk. I wonder how many times I missed entering into His Promised Inheritance for me by expecting Him to bless my plans without considering they may not necessarily be His?

There was a little hiccup when the Hebrews were ready to cross the Jordan to take possession of their promised land. The tribe of Reuben, Gad, and half the tribe of Manessah had a lot of cattle and they noticed the land of Jazer and Gilead was a good place for cattle. The grass seemed greener on the east side of Jordan than Yahweh's Promised Land for them on the westside so they took that argument to Moses.

An irate Moses took their 'better idea' of not going over Jordan but settling for what their eyes could see as their wanting to sit out the impending battles while taking their God given inheritance. This would be equally demoralizing as forty years earlier when their fathers discouraged the heart of the children of Israel from going over into this very land. It took some convincing that they would go to war with their brothers before Moses agreed that their inheritance would fall outside

God's set perimeter. But was Yahweh okay with the change of plans? Was it in the tribes of Reuben, Gad, and half of Manessah's best interest in the long run?

It's one thing to be deceived because we didn't know any better but another if we refuse to learn and obey His Teachings at all.

God said that His people would be destroyed for not seeking knowledge of His revealed will (Torah). By pridefully rejecting His knowledge He would reject them as a priestly nation. If they were choosing to forget His Torah (Teaching) then He would forget their children. (StT Hosea 4:6)

Instead of sharing the motives of revealing The Name and His Word to the world by living in unity with their brothers in the Land of Inheritance, two and a half tribes had skewed priorities by valuing their possessions more than their children. Yes, their cattle needed to be protected and fed, but they needed to protect the future of their children more.

The tribes of Reuben, Gad, and half the tribe of Manasseh should've remembered God had promised the whole nation rest from their enemies so they would dwell in safety when the Hebrews crossed *over the Jordan* to live in the land God chose for their inheritance. They also should've remembered it didn't turn out so well for Lot when he picked the rich pastureland for his cows over the hill country of Canaan. (StT Deuteronomy 12:7-10; Numbers 32:1-27; Genesis 13:10; 19:29)

But the two and a half tribes refused to keep walking *with* God in *His* direction so they essentially gave up their right to the promise of peace. This resulted in their descendants being taken captive years before the other tribes were attacked. (StT 2 Kings 15:29)

I hope no one intentionally invites disaster into their lives. It's still good to remember that to thrive and have a long life in the land of our inheritance we must not snub our noses at His Kingdom rules. It is this very substance (Torah made flesh), that restores our inner being so we can happily keep the Way of the LORD. (StT Psalms 19:8-9: 119:1)

> *"When your son asks you in time to come, "What is the meaning of the testimonies, the statutes, and the judgments, which the LORD our God has commanded you?" Then you will say to your son, we were slaves to Pharaoh in Egypt and the LORD brought us out of Egypt with a mighty hand, and the*

*LORD showed signs and wonders, great and bad upon Egypt,
upon Pharaoh, and upon all his household before our eyes.
And He brought us out from there, so He could bring us in to
give us the land which He swore to our fathers. And the LORD
commanded us to do all these statutes, to revere the LORD our
God for our good always, that He could preserve us alive, as it
is at this day. And it will be our acts of loving kindness, if we
observe to do all this commandment before the Lord our God as
He has commanded us."* (Deuteronomy 6:20-25)

Before engaging the enemy, the priest will address the troops so they will not get the heebie-jeebies at the prospect of war and seeing forces larger than theirs. After all, the One who brought them out of the land of Egypt has got this. He'll fight against their enemies to bring them victory! (StT Deuteronomy 20:1-4)

There's a Hebrew word, *Hineini,* that characterizes the response of the one being called. Usually translated as "Here I am," *hineini* is more of humbling reporting for duty with a wholehearted commitment to do whatever the *caller* asks of you; the reason you are here.

Its first recorded utterance should have been by Adam in answer to God asking where he was. Instead of repenting of walking away from the path he was created in God's image to walk, Adam made the decision not to stand in God's presence fully prepared to be dispatched.

Abraham gets credit for being the first responder to God's call even though he had no idea his 'orders' would be sacrificing his son. Thankfully, Abraham was always listening and ready to answer *"Hineini"* when another call came to stay his hand at the moment the knife was raised to cut Isaac's throat.

Both a young Samual and later Isaiah would answer God's call, *"Hineini.* Commission me!" (StT Genesis 3:9, 22:1; Isaiah 6:8)

The Lord longs to restore the intimate relationship He had always desired with man and is searching for those who will answer His summons, *"Hineini."*

Oh how I pray I will stay on high alert for His call and ready with my answer, "How may I serve You?"

Those who obey His Voice in Truth and keep His covenant, will be

His own special treasure, built into a spiritual house, a priesthood with royal authority to render a special service to Him.

You are God's choice to fully proclaim the manifestation of divine power of the One Who called you out of darkness (the reasonings of sin with its certain results) into His marvelous light.

> *Blessed and holy is the one who has a part in the first resurrection: the second death has no power to destroy them: but they will be priests of God and of the Messiah and they will reign with Him the thousand years.* (StT Exodus 19:5-6; 1 Peter 2:5, 9; Revelation 5:10, 20:6)

Priestly garments were required when ministering to the Lord. (StT Exodus 28:4)

One of the evil strategies of the accuser is to get us thinking our hand to hand combat is with people instead of him and the world rulers with the powers of darkness and the rebellious demonic forces that are holding the ignorant in bondage.

Before confronting the slanderer, we must put on our God given priestly garments so we can hold our position in the midst of the fight. This tunic has both, defensive and offensive weapons so we can successfully wage spiritual warfare. (StT Ephesians 6:11-18)

Stand prepared for victory with the belt of truth and the breastplate of righteousness. (StT Isaiah 11:5)

Declaring the Gospel of Peace enables a secure footing to walk on high places. (StT Nahum 1:15; Habakkuk 3:19)

Taking up the shield of faith empowers you to snuff out the evil one's burning arrows with its long lasting effects. (StT Deuteronomy 33:29; Proverbs 30:5)

Protect your thoughts from deception by putting on the helmet of salvation (*Yeshuah*). (StT Isaiah 59:17)

Wield the Sword of the Spirit, which is the Word of God. (StT Isaiah 11:4, 49:2; Hosea 6:5; Hebrews 4:12)

Now, even in the midst of battle, we can rejoice and keep alert in prayer on behalf of all God's consecrated people. (StT 1 Thessalonians 5:16-18)

"Behold, the days are coming, says the LORD, that I will cut a renewed covenant with the House of Israel, and with the House of Judah, not according to the covenant that I made with their fathers in the day that I took them by the hand to bring them out of the land of Egypt, My covenant which they broke, although I AM husbanding them, say the LORD. But this will be the covenant that I shall make with the House of Israel. After those days, says the LORD, I will put my Torah (Teaching) in their inward parts and write it in their hearts and I will be their God and they will be My people. And each person will no longer teach his neighbor and each person his brother saying, Know the LORD, for they all know Me from the least of them to the greatest of them, says the LORD, for I shall forgive their iniquity and I shall no longer remember their sin." (Jeremiah 31:30-33; Hebrew 8:7-12, 10:16-17)

When our blood covenant is renewed, like wedding vows, the first is not done away. It will be reaffirmed on the day the never changing Father will restore His Family of Image Keepers to His original eternal habitation: Eden. When our time of earthly exile is over, His Son will come to us keeping His promise of bringing us back home. (StT Jeremiah 29:10)

Concerning the day and hour our King will return so we can enter into His rest? No one knows, not even the Son; only the Father.

In the meantime, we are like the servants of a man who was going away to a *fur* country. But before he left, the man gave instructions for his servants to follow. Each one had an assignment that only they were to do. Then he told the gatekeeper to keep watch for the master of the house could come at midnight or at the time of the morning the Temple priest calls out. If he comes suddenly, you don't want to be found sleeping.

Since He knew we would be clueless on His actual arrival, Jesus told the disciples standing in front of Him, as well as to all of us, we must continually be on high alert! (StT Mark 13:32-37)

And it will be, if you will listen diligently to My commandments which I command you this day, to love the LORD your God, and to serve Him with all your heart and with your entire being, that I shall give you the rain of your land in its due season, the first rain and the latter rain, so you can gather in your grain, your wine, and your oil. And I will provide grass in your fields for your cattle so you can eat and be full. Take heed to yourselves, so your heart will not be deceived, and you turn aside and serve other gods and worship them. (Deuteronomy 11:13-16)

Oh for the day to be singing in His rain! All the fields will be enthusiastically rejoicing with me for He is coming! Yes, He is coming to reign with His righteous judgement and the peoples with His Truth! (StT Romans 8:18-23; Psalms 96:11-13)

Until then, I will continue to cull Sacred Cows so Jesus will not hear any mooing in my field when He suddenly opens wide the gates of His Kingdom to me. As a prisoner of hope, I can't wait to burst out of this dry constrained stall like a calf released into a lush green pasture with its refreshing cool water! Indeed, I'll be kicking up my heels as I run to my King standing in the field waiting to award me double for my shame when He restores me to Eden! (StT Zechariah 9:11-16)

Stirring the Golden Prayer Pot

Our Father, You are awe-inspiring! The great King over all the earth!

How sweet are Your words to my taste! Sweeter than honey to my mouth is the mysterious secret wisdom You planned for us before creation. The disclosure of Your Words gives light; it gives understanding to the open-minded.

Envious happiness comes to everyone who reads and puts Your prophetic Word into practice!

You renew my mind by restoring true perspective to become who You always intended me to be.

May Truth pursue me all the days of my life until You fetch me home again.

Until then, I spread a banquet of praise to You, Host Father, for Your continual feast of kept promises.

Those of us who have walked the fields with heavy hearts sowing our seeds and watering our crops with our tears, we will burst into song at harvest time! From those same long dusty rows, we will reap armloads of blessings and laugh all the way home!

We are the the people of Your pasture and we will be like crown jewels glittering over Your land.

May all of us covenanted ones be nourished by You, sitting peacefully at Your table together as part of the same family as You make Yourself available in order to bless us with Your gifts and promises.

May You place Your barbed wire fence of protection around us so all enemies cannot invade our body, soul, mind and spirit nor those of our loved ones.

May Your good pleasure continually shine upon us giving us everything needed to fulfill our purpose while supporting us with Your embrace giving us everything needed for a victorious life with complete wholeness and peace.

When these blessings come from You then our barns will overflow at harvest time, our shopping basket filled at the store, and peace and prosperity in all our undertakings.

Ingram Content Group UK Ltd.
Milton Keynes UK
UKHW010659100523
421517UK00001B/35

9 781973 656814